W9-CBS-436

The
ABINGDON
WORSHIP
ANNUAL
2009

CONTEMPORARY & TRADITIONAL
RESOURCES FOR WORSHIP LEADERS

The

ABINGDON
WORSHIP
ANNUAL
2009

EDITED BY MARY J. SCIFRES & B. J. BEU

Abingdon Press
Nashville

THE ABINGDON WORSHIP ANNUAL 2009
CONTEMPORARY AND TRADITIONAL RESOURCES FOR WORSHIP LEADERS

Copyright © 2008 by Abingdon Press

All rights reserved.

Prayers, litanies, and other worship resources in this book may be reproduced by local church congregations, provided the following credit line and copyright notice appear on all copies: From *The Abingdon Worship Annual 2009 Edition.* Copyright © 2008 by Abingdon Press. Used by permission. No other part of this work may be reproduced or transmitted in any form or by any means, electronic or mechanical, including photocopying and recording, or by any information storage or retrieval system, except as may be expressly permitted by the 1976 Copyright Act or in writing from the publisher. Requests for permission should be addressed to Abingdon Press, P.O. Box 801, 201 Eighth Avenue South, Nashville, TN 37202-0801 or e-mailed to permissions@abingdon press.com.

This book is printed on acid-free paper.

ISBN 978-0-687-65186-3

All scripture quotations unless noted otherwise are taken from the New Revised Standard Version of the Bible, copyright 1989, Division of Christian Education of the National Council of the Churches of Christ in the United States of America. Used by permission. All rights reserved.

Scripture marked Message is taken from THE MESSAGE. Copyright © Eugene H. Peterson 1993, 1994, 1995, 1996, 2000, 2001, 2002. Used by permission of NavPress Publishing Group.

Scripture quotations marked "NKJV™" are taken from the New King James Version®. Copyright © 1982 by Thomas Nelson, Inc. Used by permission. All rights reserved.

08 09 10 11 12 13 14 15 16 17—10 9 8 7 6 5 4 3 2 1

MANUFACTURED IN THE UNITED STATES OF AMERICA

To the memory of Robert E. Webber,

whose passion for God and creativity in

worship inspired so many of us who plan

Christian worship

CONTENTS

INTRODUCTION

What is worship but the proclamation of God's great worth? The words we offer in our time of worship are meaningful and important. But finding these words can be challenging and time-consuming. And so we give you *Abingdon Worship Annual 2009* as a gift of words for the art of planning worship. Here, you will find the words of many different authors, pastors, laypersons, and theologians. Some names you will recognize; others will be new to you. But each person has prayerfully studied the lections for a given worship day, focused on a theme for that day, and composed words that offer a cohesive flow for worship.

You will find liturgical resources in an order of worship for each Sunday of the lectionary year, along with suggestions for many of the "high" feast days. Each entry provides suggestions that follow an order of service that may be adapted to address your specific worship practice and format. Feel free to reorder or pick and choose the various resources to fit the needs of your worship services and congregations. Feel free, as well, to follow the suggested flow to ease your own task of planning and ordering worship.

As with *The Abingdon Worship Annual 2008*, this year's edition provides entries that follow specific thematic foci arising from one or more of the week's scriptures. This thematic focus, along with corresponding scripture imagery, is then carried out through each of the suggested prayers and litanies for a given worship service. For those who are working with contemporary worship services or who prefer more informal words, alternative ideas for those settings are offered for each service as well. Each entry includes a Call to

Worship and Opening Prayer; Prayer of Confession or Words of Assurance; Invitation or Response to the Word, Offering or Thanksgiving and Communion; and Benedictions. Additional ideas are also provided throughout this resource. We have ordered each day's suggestions to fit the basic pattern of Christian worship, reflecting a flow that leads from a time of gathering and praise, into a time receiving and responding the word, and ending with a time of sending forth. The Praise Sentences and Contemporary Gathering Words fit the spontaneous and informal nature of many nontraditional worship styles and easily fit into the time for gathering and praise. They are often designed for use in worship without a printed program or bulletin.

In response to requests from many of our readers, we have provided a number of communion liturgies as well. Some follow the pattern of the Great Thanksgiving; others are Prayers of Preparation and Consecration for the celebration of the Eucharist. Consult the index for a listing of these many communion resources, and feel free to use them interchangeably throughout the corresponding seasons.

This year, we are proud to enhance this resource with the attached CD-ROM electronic version of the full-print text. This will allow you to import printed prayers and responsive readings directly into your computer program for bulletin and program printing. With this gift of technology, we are also able to provide additional resources not found in the printed volume. For the next several years, you will find the number of electronic resources included with the *Worship Annual* increasing and expanding. In this volume, you will find an annotated bibliography of suggested websites for worship planning. You will also find a short list of suggested songs or hymns for each worship day on the CD-ROM. These suggestions are offered to streamline your worship-planning process, and we look forward to hearing from you about additional suggestions you would like to see included.

We know that *The Abingdon Worship Annual* is only one piece of the puzzle you may use for worship preparation. For additional music suggestions, you will want to consult

Prepare! A Weekly Worship Planbook for Pastors and Musicians, or *The United Methodist Music and Worship Planner,* each containing lengthy listings of lectionary-related hymns, praise songs, vocal solos, and choral anthems. As you plan lectionary-based worship, preachers will find *The Abingdon Preaching Annual* an invaluable help. Worship planners and preachers can also rely upon these three resources to provide the words, the music, and the preaching guidance to plan integrated and coordinated worship services.

All contributions in *The Abingdon Worship Annual* are based upon readings from the *Revised Common Lectionary.* As you begin your worship planning, we encourage you to spend time with the scriptures for the day, reflecting upon them thoughtfully and prayerfully. Review the thematic ideas suggested in this resource, then read through the many words for worship provided. Listen for the words that speak to you. Let this resource be the starting point for your worship planning, and allow the Spirit to guide you as God's word flows through you. Worship that arises from careful and caring planning honors the God who gave such careful planning to our creation and who gives such caring attention to our world and our needs.

Since the contributing authors represent a wide variety of denominational and theological backgrounds, the words before you will vary in style and content. Feel free to combine or adjust the words within these pages to fit the needs of your congregation and the style of your worship services. Feel free to reformat litanies into responsive format when appropriate, or to use multiple readers instead of the simple leader-congregation binary form. (Notice the reprint permission for worship given on the copyright page of this book.) Trust God's guidance, and enjoy a wonderful year of worship and praise with your congregations! We wish you God's blessings as you seek to share Christ's word and offer experiences of the Holy Spirit in your work and worship!

Mary J. Scifres and B. J. Beu, Editors

JANUARY 4, 2009

Second Sunday after Christmas/Epiphany of the Lord

Laura Jaquith Bartlett

COLOR

White

EPIPHANY SCRIPTURE READINGS

Isaiah 60:1-6; Psalm 72:1-7, 10-14; Ephesians 3:1-12; Matthew 2:1-12

THEME IDEAS

It is not unusual to see dried-out Christmas trees discarded on the curb on December 26, as people signal their readiness to be done with the trappings of the holiday. But the season is not over yet. Epiphany, the culmination of the twelve days of Christmas, comes as a wonderful gift to the church and to the world, as we eagerly turn our faces toward the glow of the star. The magi, who followed the star to Christ, thwarted Herod's treachery by taking another road home. The Light of the World illuminates that alternate path, a road of redemption from oppression and violence (Psalm 72:14). Such a beacon is not extinguished when the green and red bulbs are taken down. Celebrate Epiphany as an opportunity to follow the path of light each day of this new year.

INVITATION AND GATHERING

Call to Worship (Epiphany)

The Light of the World illuminates our path.
We have followed the star to this time of worship.
The Light of the World illuminates our way.
We have followed the star to the Christ child.
The Light of the World illuminates our lives.
We will follow Christ into a new year of living.

Opening Prayer (Epiphany, Isaiah 60)

God of the star,
    guide us as we seek to walk
        in the light and path of love.
As followers of the light,
    may we shine your glory and your justice
        into every corner of the world.
We rejoice as we claim our identity
    as people of the light.
We celebrate the brightness of your dawn!
We worship in confidence
    that you will empower and enable us
        to offer your light and your love
            to all the world.
We pray in the name of the Star-Child,
    Jesus Christ. Amen.

PROCLAMATION AND RESPONSE

Prayer of Confession (Epiphany, Matthew 2, Psalm 72)

Dear God,
    the year has just begun
        and already we are tired.
We are exhausted from the stresses
    of the holiday season.
We are burdened by the tasks
    that lie ahead in the new year.
We long for the comfort of our familiar routines,

but we're afraid of the monotony
of everyday life.
Shine your light into our world, O God!
Wake us up; shake us up;
inspire us; and energize us.
Enlighten our minds
to the possibilities for peace and justice
which your love offers.
When we take the path of least resistance,
guide our feet back to your alternate road
of love and compassion.
Illuminate the way ahead,
and open our eyes
to see the light of new possibilities.

Words of Assurance (Isaiah 60, Ephesians 3)
(Play the music to "I Want to Walk as a Child of the Light,"
quietly in the background during the prayer and assurance, then
have the congregation sing one or more stanzas as a response.)
Arise, shine, for your light has come!
The glory of the Lord has risen upon you.
The gift of God's grace is freely given for all.
The brightness of God's love forgives and sustains you.
Amen.

Passing the Peace of Christ
(To celebrate Epiphany as the culmination of the Christmas sea-
son, use the handheld candles you may have leftover from your
Christmas Eve service. Have ushers light their candles from the
Christ candle, then take the light to each pew, where worshippers
pass the light down the row, using these words:)
May the light of the world shine in your life.
We will follow the light of Christ.

Invitation to the Word
Shine the light of your word, O God,
into our lives today.
Open our eyes wide,
that we may see the brilliance of your glory.

3

Unclog our ears,
that we may hear the proclamation of your truth.
Prepare our hearts,
that we may welcome the Christ child,
the Morning star, the Prince of Peace. Amen.

THANKSGIVING AND COMMUNION

Invitation to the Offering

God sent the star to guide the magi to the Christ child.
When they encountered Jesus, they were overwhelmed
with joy and offered him their gifts. Today, Christ's light
continues to guide us, sustain us, and empower us. We,
too, are overcome with joy. We are grateful for the opportunity today, and every day, to offer our gifts to God,
claiming our identity as people of the light.

Prayer Following Communion

God of Light,
we thank you for the gifts
of bread and cup.
May we be strengthened by this meal.
May we be inspired by your light,
so that together,
we can go into the world
as followers of your path—
the path that leads to your realm
of light and glory. Amen.

SENDING FORTH

Benediction

Arise; shine, for your light has come!
God's grace sustains us.
Christ's light will illumine your path.
The Spirit's wind propels our steps.
Go forth to shine the Light into every corner of the world.
Amen!

CONTEMPORARY OPTIONS

Contemporary Gathering Words (Matthew 2)

(This is a dialogue for two persons. The first arrives via the main aisle, and the second enters by a different method, perhaps through a side door. The Christ candle should be already lit.)
Hey, where did you come from?
I took an alternate route to get here.
Well, that was unexpected!
**Yes, there are many surprises when you come
to worship God.**
How did you know how to get here?
I followed the light—it's shining for all to see.
(Together, to the congregation)
Open your eyes and follow the light!

Praise Sentences (Isaiah 60, Psalm 72, Matthew 2)

Arise; shine, for your light has come.
The glory of the Lord has risen upon you.
May the kings of Sheba and Seba,
   and the people of [*the name of your community*]
      bring gifts to the one who judges the lands
         with righteousness and justice.
Overwhelmed with joy, let us worship the Christ child!

JANUARY 11, 2009

Baptism of the Lord

Hans Holznagel

COLOR

White

SCRIPTURE READINGS

Genesis 1:1-5; Psalm 29; Acts 19:1-7; Mark 1:4-11

THEME IDEAS

The power of voice and word are coupled with the waters of creation and baptism throughout today's lections. Hovering over the waters on creation's first day, the first recorded act of God is to speak. In Psalm 29, God's voice is "over the waters," and "flashes forth flames of fire." In the wilderness, John proclaims the baptisms offered by himself and Jesus, and God's voice is heard again as John baptizes Jesus. In Acts, Paul's word is what prompts a baptism and looses the Holy Spirit in Ephesus.

INVITATION AND GATHERING

Call to Worship (Mark 1)

Wilderness water awaits us:
sweet as honey, dripping forgiveness,
wild enough to wash away wrongs.
God is there:
immersed, emerging, hovering over it,

speaking of love.
Jesus and the Spirit await us.
Come to the river of love.

Opening Prayer (Psalm 29, Mark 1)

Like restless waters on the day of creation,
    we await your presence, O God.
Touch our faces with a wind,
    gentle as night.
Thunder your word,
    clear as day.
Descend like a dove.
Help us embrace your love and goodness.
Like waters of baptism,
    make us agents of your grace,
    in Jesus' name. Amen.

PROCLAMATION AND RESPONSE

Prayer of Confession (Acts 19)

Holy Spirit, descending dove,
    you call us to follow the one
        proclaimed by John.
May our baptism be more
    than the mere water of repentance.
May it be touched
    by the fire of your presence.
As with the people of Ephesus,
    when Paul laid hands on them,
    renew and energize our faith.
Loose our tongues to speak your word—
    a prophetic word of love, hope, and justice.
Amen.

Words of Assurance (Genesis 1)

No void we can imagine is too desolate
    for God's creative power.
The one who made light and called it good
    is still the God of our evenings and mornings.

In the name of the creator of heaven and earth,
    we are forgiven.

Passing the Peace of Christ (Mark 1)

God's messengers may be wilderness prophets, familiar
friends, or strangers close at hand. As Jesus sought out
John and was blessed, let us turn to each other, offering
and receiving signs of the peace of Christ.

Response to the Word (Psalm 29, Mark 1)

Word of God, heavenly dove,
    grant us wisdom to be your people of peace.

THANKSGIVING AND COMMUNION

Invitation to the Offering (Genesis 1, Mark 1, Acts 19)

In remembrance of our call as baptized disciples, and in
gratitude for all that God has created, we bring now our
tithes and our offerings.

Offering Prayer (Genesis 1)

Maker of all good things,
    we offer back a portion of your bounty
        in these, our tithes and offerings.
Through these gifts,
    may your church embody
        your creative goodness in the world;
        in Jesus' name. Amen.

SENDING FORTH

Benediction (Mark 1)

The dove descends on you, body of Christ.
Rising from sacred waters,
    you are God's beloved, God's delight.
Go forth and be good news to the world. Amen.

CONTEMPORARY OPTIONS

Contemporary Gathering Words (Psalm 29)

Glory, strength, holy splendor, mighty power, majesty,
flashing voice, flames of fire, force of good,
give your people strength, O God.
Give your people peace.

Praise Sentences (Psalm 29, Mark 1)

Let thunderclap, whirling oak, skipping calf,
and all creation praise God.
Mighty, strange, and wonderful is our God!
Hear heavenly voices, the prophet's cry,
and roaring winds praise God.
Mighty, strange, and wonderful is our God!
Praise the creator of heaven and earth!

JANUARY 18, 2009

Second Sunday after the Epiphany

Mary J. Scifres

COLOR

Green

SCRIPTURE READINGS

1 Samuel 3:1-10 (11-20); Psalm 139:1-6, 13-18; 1 Corinthians 6:12-20; John 1:43-51

THEME IDEAS

On this ordinary Sunday, an extraordinary reminder is given in all of our scriptures: God calls us as holy and living instruments to accomplish God's work in the world. Designated as holy temples of Christ in 1 Corinthians, we follow in the lineage of Samuel, Phillip, and Nathaniel when we hear and respond to the call of God in our lives. God calls us by name: "Come and see." We hear with open hearts: "Speak, for your servants are listening." We respond with lives of service and discipleship when we follow where Christ leads.

INVITATION AND GATHERING

Call to Worship (1 Samuel 3, Psalm 139, 1 Corinthians 6, John 1)

God calls us by name, in word and in silence.
Let us listen for Christ's voice in this place.

(A time of silence may follow.)
God calls: Mary, Joseph, Michelle, Stefano,
Linda, Phillip, Pauline, Nathaniel . . .
  Speak, for your servant is listening.
From the beginning of time, God has formed us
for service, to be vessels of love in the world.
  Come and see, for Christ is shaping us still.
Christ is present within and around us,
inviting us to follow in faith and hope.
  Here we are, for Christ has called and calls us still.
Come and be the temples of God in this temple
of worship.
  May we be and become the body of Christ,
  sent into the world.

Opening Prayer (1 Samuel 3, Psalm 139)
  Speak to us, O God,
      that we might hear your call
          and respond with our lives.
  Mold us in your image.
  Fashion us for your service.
  Form us in your likeness.
  Breathe in us the Spirit of love,
      the Spirit in whom we pray. Amen.

PROCLAMATION AND RESPONSE

Call to Confession (1 Corinthians 6:12)
  Our freedom in Christ permits us to say with Paul: " 'All
  things are lawful . . . ,' but not all things are beneficial." Let
  us reflect on those things and actions in our lives that are
  not beneficial to us or to others.
  (A time of silence may follow.)

Prayer of Confession (Psalm 139, 1 Corinthians 6)
  Merciful God,
      forgive us for the many things
          that keep us from becoming
              the people you created us to be;

forgive us for the myriad ways
    we neglect your presence
        in our lives.
Clothe us with your grace
    when we stand naked before you,
    ashamed of the actions and attitudes
        that strip us of our honor and dignity.
Reform us into your likeness once again
    when we deny the imprint of your love
    and morph into people
        who ignore your image in our lives.
Reclaim us as your own
    when we drift away
        from your call in our lives.
Creator and creating God,
    mold us, remold us, hold us close,
        that we might be
            a forgiven and forgiving people.
In Christ's grace, we pray. Amen.

Words of Assurance (1 Corinthians 6)
United to Christ, through God's limitless grace,
    we become one spirit with Christ.
May that spirit be in us,
    assuring us of God's gracious forgiveness,
    both now and forevermore. Amen.

Passing the Peace of Christ (John 1)
Come and see! Christ has forgiven us!
**Let us share signs of love and forgiveness
with one another.**

Invitation to the Word (1 Samuel, Psalm 139)
Inviting God,
    speak to us now,
    that we might hear your invitation to serve.
Open our ears and our minds,
    that we might know
        your guidance and direction.

Breathe into our spirits
with your wisdom and your grace,
that we might be your loving presence
in the world.

THANKSGIVING AND COMMUNION

Invitation to the Offering (1 Samuel 3)

God has called us to lives of service.
Here I am, let it be according to your word.
Let us offer ourselves, and our gifts, with the faith
of a child.
Speak, O God, for your servant is listening.

Offering Prayer (1 Samuel 3, Psalm 139, John 1)

How wonderfully made
is your world, Creator God!
How amazing are your works
in our lives and all around us!
Transform our gifts and our giving
that what we give and who we are
may reflect your majesty and grace.
Bless our time and our talents,
that in our sharing,
others may hear your call
and know your presence.
With gratitude and joy,
we offer our prayers and our gifts. Amen.

SENDING FORTH

Benediction (1 Samuel 3, John 1)

Go into the world and speak words of love that cause ears
to tingle. Speak words of hope and faith that cause hearts
to leap. Live as ambassadors of Christ, who say, "Come
and see!" Live as followers of God who say, "Here I am!"
Speak and lead, God of grace,
for your servants are listening
and ready to follow!

CONTEMPORARY OPTIONS

Contemporary Gathering Words (1 Samuel 3)

Listen carefully! Christ is calling.
Listen carefully! God is speaking.
Listen carefully....
(A time of silence may follow.)
Respond with hope.
Here I am!
Respond with joy.
Here I am!
Respond in worship.
Here I am!

Praise Sentences (Psalm 139)

Wonderful are your works!
You made us as your own.
Wonderful are your works!
You call us as your people.
Wonderful are your works!
You live in our very lives.
Wonderful are your works!
You love us forevermore.
Wonderful are your works!

JANUARY 25, 2009

Third Sunday after the Epiphany

B. J. Beu

COLOR
Green

SCRIPTURE READINGS
Jonah 3:1-5, 10; Psalm 62:5-12; 1 Corinthians 7:29-31; Mark 1:14-20

THEME IDEAS
There is an urgency to these readings—a sense that time is short or is already at hand. Jonah prophesies to the Ninevites that they shall meet their doom at God's hands in forty days. Paul counsels the church of Corinth that time is short—indeed, the present form of this world is already passing away. And Jesus proclaims that the time is fulfilled, for the kingdom of God has come near. Whether the time is near, at hand, or seemingly over, faithful action is called for. If true faith and repentance can save Nineveh, it can save us. With the psalmist, we are called to put our faith and trust in God, who is our rock and our salvation.

INVITATION AND GATHERING

Call to Worship (Psalm 62)
For God alone our souls wait in silence.
God alone is our rock and our salvation.

In God, we shall not be shaken.
In God, we find refuge and strength.
Pour out your hearts before God.
We put our trust in God,
whose steadfast love endures forever.

Opening Prayer (Psalm 62, Mark 1)

Rock of our salvation,
remind us again
that your kingdom has come near.
Call us anew
to be your disciples,
as you called Simon and Andrew long ago.
Be our refuge and our strength
as we face the destructive forces
of our lives.
Grant us the patience
to wait for you in silence,
that we might rest secure
in your holy love. Amen.

PROCLAMATION AND RESPONSE

Prayer of Confession (1 Corinthians 7, Mark 1)

Mighty God,
we hear the words of your Son,
"The kingdom of God has come near;
repent, and believe in the good news";
but we treat it as advice to others
who are long dead.
We view the faithfulness of James and John,
who immediately left their boats to follow Jesus,
as a bewildering story
of blind trust in a complete stranger.
We imagine ourselves with their devotion,
even as we cannot find the time to study your word,
much less to have the inclination
to leave familiar paths behind.

Bless us with your steadfast love,
 that we might truly live
  as those who have seen
   your kingdom draw near. Amen.

Words of Assurance (Jonah 3, Psalm 62)

Just as God forgave the people of Nineveh
 when they repented and turned from their evil ways,
 so God will forgive us also
  when we seek forgiveness for our sins.
Pour out your hearts before God,
 who is our refuge and our strength.

Invitation to the Word (Mark 1)

Let us hear the word of God as those who know the kingdom of God has drawn near. Let us heed the word of God as those who believe in this good news. Let us live the word of God as those whose lives have been called to be a witness to others.

Call to Prayer (Psalm 62)

For God alone our souls wait in silence. For our souls are restless until they find their rest in God. Let us come before the Lord, who is our rock and our salvation. Let us find shelter in the Lord, who is our refuge and our strength. Let us pray to the One who makes all things new.

THANKSGIVING AND COMMUNION

Offering Prayer (Psalm 62, Mark 1)

God of abundance,
 you warn us against setting our hearts
  on earthly riches.
Receive these offerings
 as symbols of our faith in you
  and of your call in our lives.
May these gifts go forth
 to do your work
  in a world of misplaced faith—

a world that puts its confidence
in exploitation, deceit,
and the delusion of self-reliance. Amen.

SENDING FORTH

Benediction (Psalm 62, 1 Corinthians 7, Mark 1)

This world is passing away.
The appointed time has grown short.
We shall not be shaken.
Let us put our trust in God, who is our refuge.
Let us rest secure in God, who is our rock.
God has the power to deliver us from evil.
Believe in the good news.
The kingdom of God has come near.
God is our rock and our salvation.

CONTEMPORARY OPTIONS

Contemporary Gathering Words

Did you hear the good news?
The kingdom of God has drawn near.
Do you know who brings us this hope?
It is Jesus, the one who calls us to follow him.
Will you trust God enough to leave your former lives
behind?
**We put our faith in the Lord, our rock and our
salvation.**
Trust the Lord!
We will follow Jesus.

Praise Sentences (Psalm 62)

God is our rock.
Christ is our salvation.
The kingdom of God has come near.
God is our rock.
God is our rock.
God is our rock.

FEBRUARY 1, 2009

Fourth Sunday after the Epiphany
Erik J. Alsgaard

COLOR
Green

SCRIPTURE READINGS
Deuteronomy 18:15-20; Psalm 111; 1 Corinthians 8:1-13;
Mark 1:21-28

THEME IDEAS
Knowledge—not just what we know, but who we know
(Jesus Christ and others)—focuses today's readings. The
danger, as these texts make clear, is that a little knowledge
can be a dangerous thing. "Anyone who does not heed
the words that the prophet shall speak in my name, I my-
self will hold accountable" (Deuteronomy 18:19). How do
we know when a prophet is speaking in God's name?
How do we distinguish true from false prophesy? Psalm
111:10 offers a clue: "The fear of the LORD is the beginning
of wisdom." Paul expands this theme, noting that knowledge can be both good and bad, so be careful how you use
it. What we do with knowledge of God's purposes, and
how we respond once we come to know Jesus, makes all
the difference.

INVITATION AND GATHERING

Call to Worship (Psalm 111)

By this I have known the presence of the Lord:
in the rising of the sun,
in the smile of another's face,
in the touch of a hand
or the sound of a laugh,
in the scent of a flower
holding the promise of spring.
By this I have known the power of the Lord:
in the healing of hurts,
in the forgiveness of sin,
in the giving of gifts beyond all expectation,
in the shower of love
that comes from God's Son.
Let us give thanks to the Lord with all of our heart!
Let us worship our God, whose presence and power
endures forever!

Opening Prayer (1 Corinthians 8)

Almighty and most merciful God,
we give thanks
that you know us and love us.
Help us,
through the power of your Holy Spirit,
grow deeper, wider, and fuller
in our knowledge and understanding
of your ways.
Help us,
through the bestowal of your divine Wisdom,
bring others closer to you and to your Son,
Jesus Christ our Lord,
in whose name we pray. Amen.

PROCLAMATION AND RESPONSE

Prayer of Confession (Psalm 111)

You, God,
  are known for your wonderful deeds—
    your mercy, forgiveness, and love.
You have shown us
  the power of your works
    time and time again.
And yet,
  we are slow to comprehend;
  we refuse to acknowledge your gifts;
  we act self-sufficient,
    as if we provide ourselves everything we need,
    when we know in our hearts
    that you are the author of life.
Forgive us, we pray.
As we confess our sins,
  in thought, word or deed,
    may your redemptive presence flood our lives
    that we may praise your name forevermore. Amen.

—*Or*—

Prayer of Confession (Mark 1)

We know who you are, O Christ;
  you are the one who silences demons
    and casts out evil spirits;
  you are the one who creates new life
    out of utter chaos.
We know who you are, O Christ.
Forgive us, we pray, when we act otherwise.
In your name we pray. Amen.

Words of Assurance (Psalm 111)

God offers redemption to people of every generation,
  making new life possible for everyone.
Repent, believe in the gospel, and be healed!

Passing the Peace of Christ (Mark 1)

In meeting Christ, we become new creations. As we share the peace of Christ with each other, we share the newness of life he brings. Come, enter into new life in Christ!

Response to the Word (Mark 1, Psalm 111)

We have heard a new teaching from Jesus, this Nazarene who speaks with authority. We have seen how Christ commands even unclean spirits to flee, and they obey him. Jesus calls us to exorcise demons—in every form they take.

God of grace and God of mercy,
    grant us wisdom
        for the facing of this hour,
        and for all the hours and days
            of our lives. Amen.

THANKSGIVING AND COMMUNION

Invitation to Communion

Come, the table is set. Let us eat the food that God has prepared for us. Let us drink the wine of the new covenant. Come, the table is set. All are welcome. Come.

Great Thanksgiving (Psalm 111, Mark 1)

The Lord be with you.
    And also with you.
Lift up your hearts.
    We lift them up to the Lord.
Let us give thanks to the Lord our God.
    It is right to give our thanks and praise.
It is right, and a good and joyful thing,
    always and everywhere to give thanks to you,
    Almighty God, creator of heaven and earth.
You have created the earth and sky,
    the sea and stars,
    and all the living creatures therein.
Your works are the essence of majesty and honor.

Your righteousness lives forever.
You demonstrate your power
   in strange and unexpected ways:
   from the birth of your Son in a manger,
   to the gentle nudging of the Holy Spirit
   calling us to love one another.
The works of your hands are faithful and just,
   and your mercy endures forever.
And so, with your people on earth
   and all the company of heaven,
   we praise your name
   and join their unending hymn.
   Holy, holy, holy Lord, God of power and might,
      heaven and earth are full of your glory.
   Hosanna in the highest.
   Blessed is the one
      who comes in the name of the Lord.
   Hosanna in the highest.
Holy are you, and blessed is your Son, Jesus Christ.
   who came to cleanse us from our sins,
   and to bring us newness of life.
In the power of the Holy Spirit, he healed people,
   and taught as one who had authority.
He brought a new teaching—
   a teaching of love, forgiveness,
   and the power of God for justice and mercy.

(Words of Institution)

SENDING FORTH

Benediction (Deuteronomy 18, Mark 1)
Go on; get out of here! God's prophet, God's Son,
calls us to teach others of God's power and might.
   From this worshipping fellowship, we go into the
   community, seeking to tell others our stories.
Go on; get out of here! Share how God has transformed
you. Invite others to become disciples of this new teacher.

**We will invite others to share our journey,
even if it scares us to death.**
Go on, I mean it; get out of here! Share how God has
brought you to knowledge and wisdom of new ways,
new opportunities, new ways of being.
We go with joy. We leave in peace. Amen.

CONTEMPORARY OPTIONS

Contemporary Gathering Words (Psalm 111)
Do not fret because of all the stresses of the world!
Come, take delight in the Lord!
Leave the unpaid bills, the pile of dirty laundry,
the dirty dishes in the sink.
Come, take delight in the Lord!
Set aside the petty arguments, the backstabbing coworker,
and the person with the "I ♡ Jesus" bumper
sticker who cut you off for that last parking spot.
Now is the time! Come, take delight in the Lord!

Praise Sentences (Deuteronomy 18)
God has raised up a new prophet, filled with teachings
of love and forgiveness!
God has raised up a new prophet, Jesus the Christ!

FEBRUARY 8, 2009

Fifth Sunday after the Epiphany

B. J. Beu

COLOR

Green

SCRIPTURE READINGS

Isaiah 40:21-31; Psalm 147:1-11, 20c; 1 Corinthians 9:16-23; Mark 1:29-39

THEME IDEAS

A celebration of God's power and passion for social justice highlights each of today's readings, save the epistle. Isaiah and the psalmist proclaim that God is amazing. Have you not heard it? Have you not seen for yourself how incredible God is? God is the creator of heaven and earth. God's power is so awesome that nothing can compare to it. Yet God cares for the weakest of us. God brings the rulers of this earth to naught and rescues the downtrodden. Those who trust God will rise up with wings like eagles. Jesus, God-with-us, spent much of his ministry healing the sick and casting out afflicting demons. With the psalmist, let the church respond: "Praise the Lord!"

INVITATION AND GATHERING

Call to Worship (Isaiah 40, Psalm 147)
Have you not known? Have you not heard?
Has it not been told you from the beginning?

The Lord is the everlasting God,
the creator of heaven and earth.
God sits above the circle of the earth.
God stretches out the heavens like a curtain.
God brings princes to naught,
and makes the rulers of earth as nothing.
The Lord does not faint or grow weary.
God gives power to the weary,
and strengthens the powerless.
Those who wait for the Lord
shall renew their strength.
They shall mount up with wings like eagles.
They shall run and not be weary.
They shall walk and not faint.
Praise the Lord!
How good it is to sing praises to our God.

Opening Prayer (Isaiah 40, Psalm 147)

Everlasting God, creator of the ends of the earth,
you stretch the sky over our heads
like a canopy filled with twinkling lights.
You are great in strength
and mighty in power.
Scarcely are we sown on this earth,
scarcely do the stems of our lives take root
before the winds blow
and we are carried away like stubble
by the tempest.
Yet you care for the least of us—
healing the brokenhearted,
gathering up the outcast,
lifting up the downtrodden;
and you cast the wicked to the ground.
Renew our strength,
that we may mount up with wings like eagles,
that we may run and not be weary. Amen.

PROCLAMATION AND RESPONSE

Prayer of Confession (Isaiah 40, Psalm 147, Mark 1)

Holy God,
> we have not always lived your justice.

We have defended the privilege of the powerful,
> while ignoring the needs of the downtrodden.

We have admired the splendor of the wealthy,
> while forgetting the wonders of your creation.

Give us the heart of Jesus,
>> to care for the sick
>>> and take pity on the afflicted.

Give us the spirit of Christ,
>> to spend time in prayer
>>> and keep your path
>>>> clearly before our feet.

Give us the love of your Son,
>> to be at ease with everyone we meet,
>>> that we may truly be instruments of your grace.

Words of Assurance (Psalm 147)

The one who covers the heavens with clouds,
> prepares rain for the earth,
> makes the grass grow on the hills,
> gives animals their food,
> and takes pleasure in those who fear the Lord.

Give God the glory; sing God's praises;
> and rest secure in God's blessings.

Invitation to the Word (Psalm 147)

God does not delight in the strength of the horse, nor the speed of the runner; but takes pleasure in those who fear the Lord and whose hope is in God's steadfast love. May the words we speak and the meditation of our hearts be pleasing to God.

Call to Prayer (Isaiah 40:27, Mark 1)

Do not say with the ancient Hebrews: "My way is hidden from the LORD, and my right is disregarded by my God."

For God gives power to the faint, and strengthens the powerless. Just as Jesus went out to a deserted place to pray, let us find that quiet center in our souls and offer our prayers to God.

THANKSGIVING AND COMMUNION

Offertory Prayer (Isaiah 40, Psalm 147)
Creator of heaven and earth,
>   you bless the earth with rain,
>   make grass grow on the hills,
>   and give animals their food.
You bless us with everything we need.
Receive these offerings,
>   that they may ease the plight of the poor
>   and comfort those who are in need. Amen.

SENDING FORTH

Benediction (Isaiah 40)
Though the stress in our lives seems overwhelming,
>   **in God, we shall mount up with wings like eagles.**
Though the demands of work and family wear us out,
>   **in God, we shall run and not be weary.**
Though the injustice of this world saps our strength,
>   **in God, we shall walk and not faint.**
In God, we find steadfast love that endures forever.
Amen.

CONTEMPORARY OPTIONS

Contemporary Gathering Words (Isaiah 40, Psalm 147)
Are you tired and overworked?
>   **God lifts up the weary.**
Are you overcome with sorrow?
>   **God heals the brokenhearted.**
Are you afraid that injustice will never end?
>   **God makes the rulers of the world as nothing.**

Sing praises to our God.
Praise the Lord.

Praise Sentences (Psalm 147)

Praise the Lord!
Sing to the Lord with thanksgiving.
Make melody to our God with the lyre.
Praise the Lord!
Praise the Lord!
Praise the Lord!

FEBRUARY 15, 2009

Sixth Sunday after the Epiphany
Mary J. Scifres

COLOR
Green

SCRIPTURE READINGS
2 Kings 5:1-14; Psalm 30; 1 Corinthians 9:24-27; Mark 1:40-45

THEME IDEAS
The healing touch of God emerges as our theme in both Mark 1 and 2 Kings 5. In cleansing lepers, God reminds us that no matter how ugly our lives have become, or how devastating the diseases that haunt us, God has the power to wash us clean and offer a fresh start. Healing themes are tricky areas when faced with the very real devastation of both physical and emotional illnesses in our congregations. However, the psalmist reminds us of the Great Physician's everlasting presence, even when our lives are in the deepest places of despair.

INVITATION AND GATHERING

Call to Worship (2 Kings 5, Psalm 30)
Come to the river and pray.
Wash in the everflowing grace of God.
Come into the presence of our healing God.

Bask in the shining light of Christ's love.
Come as you are; be where you are;
but know that God is all around.

Opening Prayer (2 Kings 5, Psalm 30)

God of health and wholeness,
    embrace us,
        even in our brokenness.
Wash us with your loving presence.
Cleanse our ears,
    that we may hear you plainly.
Cleanse our hearts,
    that we may love you fully.
Cleanse our lives,
    that we may walk with joy
        and sing your praises.

PROCLAMATION AND RESPONSE

Prayer of Confession (2 Kings 5, Mark 1)

God of everflowing grace,
    wash over us with your mercy.
Overwhelm us with floods of love.
Cleanse us and make us new.
As we come into your presence,
    remind us of our baptism
        that we may be thankful.
Help us sense anew
    the power of your baptismal presence.
Open our hearts to the fullness of your grace
    as we confess our brokenness and our sins.
Heal us of our pain and despair,
    our resistance to finding rest in your presence,
    our agonies that prevent us
        from feeling your loving touch.
(Silent Prayer)

Words of Assurance (Psalm 30)

Weeping may linger for the night,
    but joy comes with the morning.

The grace of God is ours for the taking!
Put off the sackcloth and ashes of despair,
  and dance in the light of God's love.
In the name of Christ, we are forgiven!

Passing the Peace of Christ
Forgiven and reconciled to God, let us now share signs of
reconciliation and love with one another.

THANKSGIVING AND COMMUNION

Invitation to the Offering (2 Kings 5, Mark 1)
As Christ has given grace to us, so now we are invited to
share God's grace with others. Let us open our hearts and
our lives, that others may know the healing power of God.

Prayer of Thanksgiving (Psalm 30, Mark 1)
Loving God,
    we praise you and thank you
      for the many gifts
        of gracious healing in our lives.
We sing of your mighty works,
    and we proclaim your healing power
      as we share our gifts with others.
Like the leper who could not keep silent,
    may we sing loudly and shout your praises
      in all that we say and all that we do!

SENDING FORTH

Benediction (2 Kings 5, Psalm 30, Mark 1)
God has established you as a mighty mountain.
    We will not be silent.
God has healed you with mercy and love.
    We will not be silent.
Sing of God's love and shout of Christ's grace.
    We will sing and shout with love and joy!

CONTEMPORARY OPTIONS

Contemporary Gathering Words (2 Kings 5, Psalm 30)
Trade your sorrows for joy and love.
   Yes, God!
Trade your sins for mercy and grace.
   Yes, God!
Trade your fears for confidence and hope.
   Yes, God!
Trade your sorrows for joy and love.
   Yes, God!

Praise Sentences (Psalm 30)
Sing praises to God.
Give thanks to the Lord.
   Sing praises to God.
   Give thanks to the Lord.

FEBRUARY 22, 2009

Transfiguration Sunday
Bryan Schneider-Thomas

COLOR
White

SCRIPTURE READINGS
2 Kings 2:1-12; Psalm 50:1-6; 2 Corinthians 4:3-6; Mark 9:2-9

THEME IDEAS
Today's readings reveal God coming into the world. Each text presents a variation of the idea that God is active in the world and in the lives of the faithful. When this happens, it may leave us a bit awestruck or even dumbstruck. These readings also present an important vocal component: Elijah and Elisha's conversation culminates in the transfer of power from the master to the pupil; the psalm proclaims that God does not keep silent; Paul acknowledges that we must proclaim Jesus Christ; and in contrast, Jesus instructs the disciples to keep silent about him until the proper time.

INVITATION AND GATHERING

Call to Worship (Psalm 50, 2 Corinthians 4)
Cry out!
    God does not keep silent.

Cry out!
We long to hear God's word.
Cry out!
Tell of God's wonderful deeds.

Opening Prayer (2 Corinthians, Mark 9)

Almighty God, giver of life,
your light shines in our lives
and your glory is revealed
through your Son, Jesus Christ.
Reveal his glory to us
as you did to Peter, James, and John,
that we may be filled with his power
and our mouths may proclaim his presence
forevermore. Amen.

PROCLAMATION AND RESPONSE

Prayer of Confession

Mighty one of yesterday, today, and tomorrow,
do not be silent, but speak, that we may hear.
Speak justice, that we may correct our lawlessness.
Speak righteousness, that we may know your ways.
Speak compassion, that we may know your mercy.
Speak abundance, that we may serve others.
Speak understanding, that we may be peacemakers.
Speak glory, that we may know your Son.
Speak, and we will listen to you.
You promise forgiveness of sins and fullness of grace
when we speak our shortcomings.
We speak of mistakes we have made.
We speak of abandoning your ways.
We speak of failures to show compassion and mercy.
We speak of our need for forgiveness.
Mighty one of yesterday, today, and tomorrow,
hear our prayer and lead us into fullness of life. Amen.

Words of Assurance

God will not keep silent, but will gather us in
with the tender words: "You are forgiven."
Glory to God!

Passing the Peace of Christ

As Elisha would not leave Elijah,
may God forever keep us close in Christ.
The peace of Christ be with you always.
And also with you.

Response to the Word (Mark 9)

As they were coming down the mountain, Jesus ordered
his disciples to tell no one about what they had seen,
for his time was not at hand.
**How can we keep silent when we have seen what we
have seen and heard what we have heard? Will not
the heavens proclaim it? Will not the earth
announce such news?**
Yes, now is the day and now is the time, for Jesus Christ
has died and is raised in glory.
**Shout it to the highest mountain and announce it in
the lowest valley: Jesus Christ, the glory of God, the
Son of righteousness, the Prince of Peace, is here!**

THANKSGIVING AND COMMUNION

Invitation to the Offering

We proclaim Jesus Christ with our mouths, in our actions,
and through our lives. Let us offer up our lives to Christ,
that in our lives we may be servants of Jesus Christ.

Offering Prayer

Lord Jesus,
all that we have is yours,
and all that we are is yours.
In offering these tokens of our lives,
may all that we do
serve you to the glory of God. Amen.

SENDING FORTH

Benediction
Cry out!
God's word has been spoken.
Cry out!
Our hearts are filled with praise.
Cry out!
Our lives proclaim God's glory.
Cry out the bounty of God's love.

CONTEMPORARY OPTIONS

Contemporary Gathering Words
(The response of "Jesus Christ" may be spoken in normal vol-
ume, or it may be whispered initially, increasing in volume each
time it is spoken.)
Come to the light—
Jesus Christ
Come to the glory—
Jesus Christ
Come to the Word—
Jesus Christ
Come and worship—
Jesus Christ
Come and sing—
Jesus Christ
Come and praise—
Jesus Christ!

Praise Sentences
Shout out loud!
Sing with joy!
Rejoice with gladness!
Announce that the glory of God is here.

FEBRUARY 25, 2009

Ash Wednesday
B. J. Beu

COLOR
Purple

SCRIPTURE READINGS
Joel 2:1-2, 12-17; Psalm 51:1-17; 2 Corinthians 5:20b–6:10;
Matthew 6:1-6, 16-21

THEME IDEAS
Ash Wednesday begins the journey of Lent—the journey
of following Jesus' steps to Jerusalem, the journey of turn-
ing toward the cross. Ash Wednesday begins a period of
introspection—a time to reflect upon what it means to be
a Christian and to take up one's cross and to follow Jesus.
The imposition of ashes on our foreheads reminds us of
the frailty of our lives here on earth. We were created out
of the dust, and to dust we shall return. Divine judgment
is at hand, but this judgment is tempered with mercy and
a call to begin our journey anew. Ash Wednesday presents
the promise and hope of salvation when we return to God.

INVITATION AND GATHERING

Call to Worship (Joel 2)
Blow the trumpet in Zion.
Sound the alarm on God's holy mountain!

**The day of the Lord draws near—
a day of darkness and gloom.**
Yet even now, who knows if God will relent,
and turn our calamity into joy.
**Let us rend our hearts, not our clothing, and return
to the Lord, who abounds in steadfast love.**
Let us forsake the ways that lead to death,
and return to God with all our hearts!
**Have mercy on us, O God,
and save us from our iniquities.**

Opening Prayer (Joel 2)
God of dust and ash,
  you fashioned us from the dust of the earth,
    and to dust we shall return.
May the ashes placed upon our foreheads this day
  remind us of who we are,
    and whose we are.
Draw us back to you, O God,
  for you are gracious and merciful,
    slow to anger, and abounding in steadfast love.
Heal the hardness of our hearts,
  that we may be faithful disciples
    of the one who makes all things new. Amen.

PROCLAMATION AND RESPONSE

Prayer of Confession (Psalm 51)
Holy God,
  wash us thoroughly of our iniquity
    and cleanse us from our sin.
For our transgressions are ever before us,
  and we have done what is evil in your sight.
You desire truth in our inward being,
  yet we turn our back on the wisdom
    you would impart in our hearts.
Create in us a clean heart, O God,
  and put a new and right spirit within us.

Do not cast us away from your presence,
and do not take your Holy Spirit from us.
Forgive our sins,
and lead us in your paths anew,
that we might teach transgressors your ways
and lead sinners to return to you. Amen.

Words of Assurance (Joel 2:12-13)

Hear the words of the prophet Joel: "Yet even now, says the LORD, / return to me with all your heart, / with fasting, with weeping, and with mourning; / rend your hearts and not your clothing. / Return to the LORD, your God, / for [God] is gracious and merciful, / slow to anger, and abounding in steadfast love, / and relents from punishing."

Invitation to the Word

Just as the ashes we place upon our foreheads remind us of the frailty of our lives here on earth, and of our need to live each day to the fullest, may these readings prepare our hearts to face our mistakes and to commit ourselves to leading more godly lives.

Call to Prayer (Matthew 6)

God, who dwells in secret, hears the prayers of our hearts and the yearnings of our spirit. Let us enter into silent prayer to the One who sees in secret and rewards the humble of heart.

THANKSGIVING AND COMMUNION

Offering Prayer (Matthew 6)

Gracious God,
we have sought recognition for our piety
and taken pride in our giving,
congratulating ourselves
for caring about our neighbors.
Receive these offerings,
in the spirit of your Son,

who taught us that where our heart is,
    there our treasure will be also. Amen.

SENDING FORTH

Benediction (Psalm 51)
Wash us thoroughly from our iniquities
and we will be whiter than snow.
Bathe us in your steadfast love.
Create in us a clean heart, O God,
and help us hear the joy of your calling.
Restore to us the joy of your salvation.
Go with God's blessing.

CONTEMPORARY OPTIONS

Contemporary Gathering Words (Joel 2, Psalm 51)
We have made a mess of our lives.
Wash away our sin, O God!
We have turned our back on the truth of your salvation.
Don't send us away from your presence!
We have come to turn from our destructive habits.
Put your Holy Spirit within us!

Praise Sentences (2 Corinthians 5)
Christ came to reconcile us with God.
God be praised!
Christ came for our salvation.
Christ be praised!
Christ came to make us holy.
The Spirit be praised!

MARCH 1, 2009

First Sunday in Lent
Mary J. Scifres

COLOR
Purple

SCRIPTURE READINGS
Genesis 9:8-17; Psalm 25:1-10; 1 Peter 3:18-22; Mark 1:9-15

THEME IDEAS
As we move into the season of Lent, we embark upon a journey—a journey with our ancient Hebrew sisters and brothers, as we recall the history of God's covenant with humanity through Noah, Abraham, Moses, and Jeremiah. We embark upon a journey with Christ through the wilderness of our lives, with its many temptations on the road to death and resurrection. Journeying toward Easter, we encounter God's promises of hope and life; we encounter our role to bring this message of hope to others.

INVITATION AND GATHERING

Call to Worship (Mark 1)
Good news is at hand.
God calls us this day.
  Repent and believe.
  Trust in the goodness of God.
Good news is at hand.

God calls us this day.
Turn from death and despair.
Turn from tempation and sin.
Good news is at hand.
God calls us this day.
The time is fulfilled.
God's kingdom is near.
Good news is at hand.
God's kingdom is here.

Opening Prayer (Genesis 9, Psalm 25)
Loving God,
we lift up our souls
and search for your promised presence.
Reveal yourself to us this day—
in mighty mountains, in brilliant rainbows,
in curious creatures, in spring rain showers,
in joyous children, in grieving friends,
in challenging scriptures, in meaningful prayers,
in repentances and forgiveness, in love and grace.
Teach us your ways.
Lead us in your truth.
Guide us on the Lenten journey
toward the darkness of death
and the hope of resurrection.
In the name of the risen Christ, we pray. Amen.

PROCLAMATION AND RESPONSE

Call to Confession
Repent and believe; the time is fulfilled. God's realm is
near; Christ is present with us now. Come! Bring your confession before God.
(Time of silent confession or reflection)

Prayer of Confession (Psalm 25)
God of hope and help,
show us your ways.
Lead us in your truth.

43

Do not remember the sins of our youth,
    or the sins of this past week.
Even as we remember the error of our ways,
    we ask for your forgiveness
       and your grace.
Help us know you so completely
    that we may walk in your paths
       of love and righteousness,
          and live in the light of your grace.

Words of Assurance (1 Peter 3)

Christ carries our sins
    on the wings of God's love and grace.
Once, for all, Christ has suffered,
    that our sins may be put to death
       and our lives may be given new birth.
What God has put to death,
    let us now put to death.
In the name of Christ,
    we are forgiven!
In the name of God,
    we are alive in the Spirit!

Passing the Peace of Christ (Genesis 9)

As symbols of the new covenant of love that Christ has written upon our hearts, let us share together signs of love and peace.

Prayer of Preparation (Psalm 25)

God of wisdom and truth,
    teach us your ways.
As we hear the words of your promise,
    and as we reflect on the message you offer,
    let us hear your voice.
Lead us in your truth
    and teach us to be your people.
In Christ's name, we pray. Amen.

THANKSGIVING AND COMMUNION

Invitation to the Offering or Invitation to Communion (Genesis 9)

Christ has offered his very self to us. Let us open ourselves to God, that we may experience the presence of Christ fully. Let us offer ourselves to God, that others may experience Christ through our presence in God's world.

Offering Prayer (Genesis 9)

In gratitude and praise,
    we remember the many gifts of your creation
        and of your covenant with us.
Accept these gifts we bring,
    that others may find in them
        signs of your love and grace.
Gather these gifts
    and the gifts of our lives.
Color them with hope and joy,
    that in our giving and in our living,
        a brilliant rainbow of love may shine forth.
In Christ's name, we pray.

SENDING FORTH

Benediction (Genesis 9)

Go forth as signs of God's love.
    We go as rainbows of hope and grace.
Go forth as children of the promise.
    We go as signs of God's love!

CONTEMPORARY OPTIONS

Contemporary Gathering Words (Genesis 9, Mark 1, Lent)

A rainstorm, a flood, a boat, and a promise from God.
A rainbow, a dove, a sign of this promise.
A river, a cousin, a baptism, and a promise from God.
A revelation, a journey, a ministry, a sign of this promise.

On this day, we remember signs of the past,
    but also promises for the future.
On this day, we embark on a journey ancient as the earth,
    but refreshing as spring rain.
On this day, we move closer to the cross,
    closer to death, closer to resurrection, closer to Christ.
All are part of this journey of living, experiencing,
    and being the promises of God.

Praise Sentences (Mark 1)
The time is fulfilled.
God's realm has come near.
Sing praises to Christ, the promise of God!

MARCH 8, 2009

Second Sunday in Lent
Mary Petrina Boyd

COLOR
Purple

SCRIPTURE READINGS
Genesis 17:1-7, 15-16; Psalm 22:23-31; Romans 4:13-25;
Mark 8:31-38

THEME IDEAS
Risk and promise unite these texts. God made a covenant
with Abraham, who risked all he had to be faithful. Paul
refers to that covenant as he talks about the righteousness
of faith and God's promise. Jesus reminds us that those in
the covenant community may face suffering. He invites
his followers to risk all they have to live in faith and fully
experience the blessings of the covenant.

INVITATION AND GATHERING

Call to Worship (Psalm 22, Romans 4)
Let all the ends of the earth return to God.
    We give glory to God, who is worthy of praise!
Let all the families of the world worship God.
    We praise the Lord, who promises life to all!
Let all the people of God rejoice together.
    We worship and adore our God.

Opening Prayer (Genesis 17)

God of promise,
    we come as your people,
        rejoicing in the abundance of your love.
Give us faith to answer your call.
Strengthen us to hope against hope.
Guide us into a deep and abiding trust.
Lead us on a journey toward wholeness,
    that we may become your holy people,
        faithfully doing your will. Amen.

PROCLAMATION AND RESPONSE

Prayer of Confession (Mark 8)

Gracious God,
    we want to hold on
        to what we know;
    we are afraid to take risks
        for the sake of the gospel;
    we want to keep our lives safe.
Forgive us, O God,
    when we cling to comfort,
    when we build barriers
        to protect ourselves,
    when we chose the easy way.
Transform our fears,
    that we may deny ourselves,
    take up our cross,
        and follow Jesus
        to serve the world. Amen.

Words of Assurance (Mark 8, Romans 4)

Those who risk their lives for the sake of Jesus Christ
    will inherit the world.

Passing the Peace of Christ (Genesis 17, Romans 4)

God invites us into a covenant of grace. We inherit God's
promise, for we are all God's children. Greet your sisters
and brothers with the peace of Christ.

Response to the Word *(Genesis 17, Romans 4, Mark 8)*

God of the journey,
let your word guide our ways.
May the abundance of your promises
strengthen our faith,
that we may follow you,
even at the risk of losing earthly treasures
for the sake of your eternal realm. Amen.

THANKSGIVING AND COMMUNION

Invitation to the Offering *(Mark 8, Psalm 22)*

Those who want to save all they have will lose everything, while those who give all they are for the sake of Jesus Christ, will gain eternal blessing. Come, bring what you have and offer it to God, that the poor will have food in abundance, and all may know God's love.

Offering Prayer *(Genesis 17, Romans 4, Mark 8)*

God of the ages,
from generation to generation
you have blessed us
with life and abundant love.
We have a rich inheritance of faith.
Use the gifts we bring
to restore hope to the hopeless
and faith to those who despair.
We would give what we have
that we may follow you
with all our heart. Amen.

SENDING FORTH

Benediction *(Genesis 17, Romans 4)*

Grow strong in faith as you glorify God.
Live in the assurance of God's promises.
May the abundance of God's blessings
be with you now and forever.

CONTEMPORARY OPTIONS

Contemporary Gathering Words (Psalm 22)
God has done it!
What has God done?
God has delivered us!
What shall we do?
Let us praise God!
May our hearts praise God forever!

Praise Sentences (Psalm 22)
Our God is awesome!
Give God the glory!
Praise God with joy,
and serve God always!

MARCH 15, 2009

Third Sunday in Lent
Robert Blezard

COLOR
Purple

SCRIPTURE READINGS
Exodus 20:1-17; Psalm 19; 1 Corinthians 1:18-25; John 2:13-22

THEME IDEAS
The story of God's saving revelation is at the heart of the lectionary readings. The Decalogue in Exodus lifts up God's gift of the law of Moses, through which Jews found righteousness. The psalm heralds God's law: perfect, enlightening, and life-giving. But Paul tells the churches at Corinth that while the Jews still look to the law, the fullness of God's salvation is revealed in the gospel. In John, Jesus' action and prophecy in the temple courtyard underscores the notion that, with Christ, we have the fullness and successor to the law.

INVITATION AND GATHERING

Call to Worship (Psalm 19)
Weary and overwhelmed, we gather.
God's holy word revives us.
Simple and confused, we yield.

God's word gives us wisdom.
Blind and uncomprehending, we await.
God's word enlightens our eyes.
More precious than gold is God's word.
Sweeter than honey are God's commands.

Opening Prayer (1 Corinthians 1, John 2)

O God,
>your weakness is mightier than human strength,
>your foolishness is wiser than human wisdom.

We rejoice that you are with us today.
Open our hearts and discipline our will.
Teach us to follow your perfect ways.
Test us with your righteous decrees.
As with a whip,
>drive us from unholy living,
>>and turn us toward your holy light.

Through your Son, Jesus Christ,
>comfort and redeem us with your holy gospel.

PROCLAMATION AND RESPONSE

Prayer of Confession (Psalm 19, John 2)

With hearts of sorrow,
>we come before you, O God,
>>to confess what you already know—
>>>we have failed to keep your laws.

Again and again,
>we have followed our own selfish will,
>>rather than your holy and life-giving will
>>>for our lives.

We have twisted your decrees and institutions
>to suit our preconceptions and interests
>>rather than your own.

Forgive us, O God,
>and cleanse us from hidden faults,
>that the words of our mouths,
>>and the meditations of all our hearts,

52

may be acceptable to you,
our Rock and our Redeemer.

Words of Assurance (Exodus 20)
God shows steadfast love
and blesses to the thousandth generation
those who walk in God's ways.
In love, God sent Jesus
to bless and redeem God's people.
God forgives us our sins
and restores us to new life.
Let us rejoice in God's mercy.

Passing the Peace of Christ (Exodus 20, 1 Corinthians 1)
The Lord continues to bring God's people from slavery
into freedom. Through the power of the cross of Christ,
we are being saved. May the peace of Christ be with you.
And also with you.
Let us share signs of peace with one another.

Invitation to the Word (Psalm 19)
The universe proclaims God's truth.
God's knowledge flows night and day!
**We open our ears to hear, our minds
to comprehend, our hearts to receive.**

Response to the Word (John 2)
Holy and eternal God, you make foolish
the wisdom of the world.
**Through the foolishness of the cross,
you save those who believe.**
Help us, O God, believe not only with our lips
but also with our lives.
Amen.

THANKSGIVING AND COMMUNION

Invitation to the Offering (Psalm 19, John 2)
We worship a God of abundance,
from whose hands flow all the blessings of our lives.

May we be spared the sin of using these blessings
   simply for our own pleasure and purposes.
Give us right and generous hearts, O God,
   that your blessings may flow from our hands
      to those in need.

Offering Prayer (1 Corinthians 1)

The wisdom of the world
   tells us to hoard what we own, O God,
      while you invite us to share what we have
      with those in need.
Accept these gifts for your purposes,
   that we may be your servants in the world.

SENDING FORTH

Benediction (1 Corinthians 1)

We proclaim the crucified and risen Christ,
who is the power and wisdom of God.
   May Christ strengthen us and give us wisdom.
Go forth in the name of Christ!
   Amen!

CONTEMPORARY OPTIONS

Contemporary Gathering Words (Psalm 19, 1 Corinthians 1)

The world finds no proof of God.
   But the heavens tell of God's glory.
God's message is foolishness to the world.
   But God's folly trumps human wisdom.
The freedom of the world brings us death.
   But obedience to God's ways brings life.
We gather in the name of Christ crucified.
   The Word made flesh brings life to God's people!

Praise Sentences

When we open our eyes, we see your glory, O God.
   Sun, moon, and stars proclaim your magnificence.

When we open our ears, we hear your word, O God.
The voice of creation reaches the ends of the earth.
When we open our hearts, we receive your truth, O God.
You fill us with joy and light forever.
When we open ourselves, we praise your holy name.
Praise God's holy name.

MARCH 22, 2009

Fourth Sunday in Lent/One Great Hour of Sharing

Jamie D. Greening

COLOR

Purple

SCRIPTURE READINGS

Numbers 21:4-9; Psalm 107:1-3, 17-22; Ephesians 2:1-10; John 3:14-21

THEME IDEAS

God's love for humanity explodes like light from a supernova in these lections. In these readings, we hear three phrases that paint the backdrop for God's saving action: "For God so loved the world" (John 3:16), "his steadfast love endures forever" (Psalm 107:1b), and "out of the great love with which he loved us" (Ephesians 2:4-5). Even the Mosaic story of the serpents in Numbers serves as a prelude for the loving mission of Jesus Christ when the battered Savior is lifted up on a rapidly approaching Good Friday. Yet, for love to be fully realized, it demands a response. The appropriate response to God's love is faith. Jesus calls on us to believe, and the psalmist reminds us that faith is often the action of knowing from whom to ask for help, as the Israelites "cried to the LORD in their

trouble, / and he saved them from their distress" (Psalm
107:19).

INVITATION AND GATHERING

Call to Worship (Psalm 107, Ephesians 2, John 3)
God loves us with a steadfast love.
Let the redeemed of the Lord say so!
God loves us so much he gave us his Son.
Let us believe and have eternal life!
God loves us with a great love, rich in mercy.
Let us have faith to receive this grace!
Give thanks to the Lord, for God is good.

Opening Prayer (John 3, Ephesians 2)
Great Triune God,
 we have gathered here in your name
  as an act of faith,
   believing that you are not only among us,
    but that you love us.
It is often hard to recognize your love,
 see your mercy, and feel your presence.
Help us today in our worship,
 that we might be transparent to your grace,
  as you reveal yourself to each one of us. Amen.

PROCLAMATION AND RESPONSE

Prayer of Confession (Numbers 21)
God, we have sinned against you.
We have spoken against you and your servant Jesus.
We have uttered lies.
We have cursed you and others.
We have said vulgar things.
We have been consumed by doubt.
We have been bitten with the venom of hatred
 in our world.
We have oppressed the helpless.
We have been intolerant of others.

We have delighted in violence.
We have spent money foolishly.
Please, Lord God, forgive us our transgressions,
that we may be healed of our sin.

Words of Assurance (John 3)
Hear now the loving truth of God:
   God did not send the Son into the world
     to condemn the world,
      but that the world might be saved through him.
   Those who believe in him are not condemned.

Passing the Peace of Christ (Psalm 107)
(Divide the congregation into sections to announce the Passing *of the Peace.)*
Around us, our brothers and sisters are gathered:
   from the east,
   from the west,
   from the north,
   from the south.
Share the steadfast love of God and community
as the peace of God is passed.

Response to the Word (Ephesians 2)
We have heard the word of God—
the word of love.
   Lord, have mercy.
We have heard the word of God—
the word of grace.
   Christ, have mercy.
We have heard the word of God—
the word of service and ministry.
   Lord, have mercy.

Introduction to the Sermon
To preach the love of God is to preach the heart of God.
Whether our message addresses ministry to the sick,
global missions, evangelism, social justice, or family issues, this message is always rooted in God's love, or it is
not rooted in God. May the Holy Spirit open up our

innermost being to what God wants most: to give love to us and to receive love from us.

THANKSGIVING AND COMMUNION

Invitation to the Offering (Psalm 107, Ephesians 2)
We are created in Christ Jesus for good works, and this is his gift to us. Let us now do the loving, good work of giving our gifts back to him. Let us bring our gifts of thanksgiving to celebrate his deeds and his wonderful works to humankind.

Litany of Thanksgiving (Psalm 107, John 3)
Give thanks to the Lord, for God is good.
  God's steadfast love in Christ endures forever.
Give thanks to the Lord, for God is good.
  God's steadfast love gave us salvation
  through Jesus Christ, our Lord.
Give thanks to the Lord, for God is good.
  God's steadfast love has not left us to perish.
Give thanks to the Lord, for God is good.
  God's steadfast love provides eternal life.
Give thanks to the Lord, for God is good.

SENDING FORTH

Benediction (Ephesians 2)
God's great love and rich mercy
  have made us alive in Christ.
Let us depart to live lives of grace,
  and to do good works.

CONTEMPORARY OPTIONS

Contemporary Gathering Words (John 3)
For God so loved *(name of church or faith community)*
  that God gave his only child, Jesus Christ,
  so that any human being,
  of any background,

who believes in the mission,
work, and atonement in Christ
will not suffer punishment,
but instead have the gift
of eternal joy and life.

Praise Sentences (Ephesians 2)

God's great love is amazing.
Amazing love makes God great.
God's great love is amazing.

MARCH 29, 2009

Fifth Sunday in Lent

B. J. Beu

COLOR

Purple

SCRIPTURE READINGS

Jeremiah 31:31-34; Psalm 51:1-12; Hebrews 5:5-10; John 12:20-33

THEME IDEAS

The theme of renewal unites these readings. The prophet Jeremiah proclaims that the days are coming when God will make a new covenant with the people Israel—a covenant written on their hearts. The psalmist cries out to be washed clean and to have a new spirit placed within the human heart. Jesus proclaims that this renewal requires sacrifice, even death—for unless a grain of wheat dies, it yields no fruit. The author of Hebrews maintains that Christ has made the sacrifice necessary for this renewal in our lives.

INVITATION AND GATHERING

Call to Worship (Jeremiah 31, Psalm 51:10-12)
Come! Cry out with the psalmist:
"Create in me a clean heart, O God,
and put a new and right spirit within me."

Write your laws upon our hearts, O Lord,
and we will be your people.
**"Do not cast me away from your presence,
and do not take your holy spirit from me."**
Be our God, and we will be your people.
**"Restore to me the joy of your salvation,
and sustain in me a willing spirit."**

Opening Prayer (John 12:24 NKJV™)
God of renewal,
though Jesus' soul was troubled,
he followed your ways
with poise and purpose.
Opening our eyes to your glory,
Jesus taught us to see past our fears—
to face death and the unknown, unafraid:
"Most assuredly, I say to you,
unless a grain of wheat
falls into the ground and dies,
it remains alone;
but if it dies, it produces much grain."
Help us bear the fruit of new life,
that you may be glorified,
and that all people
may come to know your ways. Amen.

PROCLAMATION AND RESPONSE

Prayer of Confession (Jeremiah 31, Psalm 51)
Renew us, Lord;
wash us of our wickedness
and cleanse us from our sin.
Put your law within us
and write it on our hearts.
Take away our excuses,
our protestations of ignorance,
our pathetic insistence
that we did not properly understand

what we were doing.
We long for the day
  when we will not feel compelled
    to beg excuses for our deeds.
Create in us a clean heart, O God,
  and put a new and right spirit within us.
Do not cast us away from your presence
  and do not take your Holy Spirit from us.

Response to the Word (Jeremiah 31, John 12)

Through the life, death, and resurrection of Jesus,
  God has written the law of life on our hearts.
No longer need we teach one another
    truths uttered of old,
  for God has placed the ways of life and death
    in our inward being.
May we live as those who know the Lord!

Call to Prayer (John 12)

Jesus prayed that God's name would be glorified and it was glorified. We pray that our lives may be reflections of Jesus' love and grace and it is so. Let us bring our prayers before the Lord, that God may be glorified, and we may be heirs of salvation with Christ.

THANKSGIVING AND COMMUNION

Invitation to the Offering (Jeremiah 31)

The God who led the Hebrew people by the hand out of Egypt, the God who gave our ancestors the laws of life and made covenant with them, has blessed us with a new covenant written on our very hearts. Let us respond with thankfulness as we offer our tithes and offerings back to God this day.

SENDING FORTH

Benediction (John 12)

Death has lost its sting.
In Christ, we bear much fruit.

Death has lost its sting.
In Christ, we are reflections of God's glory.
Death has lost its sting.
In Christ, we are renewed and made whole.
Go with God's blessing.

CONTEMPORARY OPTIONS

Contemporary Gathering Words (Psalm 51)

We feel old and worn out.
Renew us, Lord.
The mistakes of our past stain us like ground-in grime.
Wash away our sin.
Purge us of our evil thoughts and ways.
Make us whiter than snow.
Don't send us away from your presence!
Put your Holy Spirit within us!

Praise Sentences (John 12)

Glorify your name, O God.
God responds, "I have glorified it."
Glorify your name, O God.
God proclaims, "Christ has glorified it."
Glorify your name, O God.
God challenges, "You glorify it."
We glorify your name, O God!

APRIL 5, 2009

Passion/Palm Sunday
Mary J. Scifres

COLOR
Purple

PALM SUNDAY SCRIPTURE READINGS
Psalm 118:1-2, 19-29; Mark 11:1-11

PASSION SUNDAY SCRIPTURE READINGS
Isaiah 50:4-9a; Psalm 31:9-16; Philippians 2:5-11; Mark 14:1–15:47 or Mark 15:1-39 (40-47)

THEME IDEAS
From passion to promise, Holy Week takes us through a long and arduous journey. Oddly enough, we begin with palms—promises of life and hope—even as we prepare to endure the agony of betrayal, despair, and death.

INVITATION AND GATHERING

Call to Worship (Mark 11, Psalm 118)
This day is the Lord's, created for joy.
Let us rejoice and be glad in it!
Hosanna to Christ, the blessed child of God.
Hosanna to God in the highest!
Blessed is the one who comes in God's name.
Hosanna to God in the highest!

This day is the Lord's, created for love.
Let us rejoice and be glad in it!

Opening Prayer (Psalm 118, Philippians 2)

God of grace and glory,
blessed is your Son, Christ Jesus,
and blessed is your holy name.
As we bless your name and sing with joy,
awaken our ears to hear your word;
awaken our hearts to listen for your wisdom.
As we rejoice in this day that you have made,
help us hear even the hard news
of Christ's suffering and death.
As we celebrate your presence with palms and praises,
guide us to live your teachings,
even when the path is painful and difficult.
May your presence flow through us
into your world.
In the name of your Son, Christ Jesus, we pray.

PROCLAMATION AND RESPONSE

Call to Confession (Philippians 2)

At the name of Jesus, may every knee bend, every tongue confess, and every soul trust that Jesus Christ is Lord and Savior of us all. In trust and hope, let us confess our sins before God.

Prayer of Confession (Psalm 31, Mark 14–15)

Gracious God,
you know our every sorrow,
our every need.
Hear us as we remember the times
when our strength failed us,
when our distress led us onto paths
of hopelessness and despair.
Forgive us when we betray you,
when we deny you,
when we deride you, or mock you.

Awaken in us a new resolve
  to be aware of your call
    and presence in our lives.
Help us stay awake,
  even when the days are hard
    and the nights are long.
Strengthen us to trust in you
  and to walk with you,
    even on this path to the cross.
Let your face shine upon us,
  that we may know your steadfast love
    and trust in your resurrection promises.
In Christ's name, we pray.

Words of Assurance (Psalm 31, Philippians 2)

Know that the Lord is God,
  and that Christ's face shines upon us
    even when we turn away from God's brightness.
Walk in the light, dear friends.
Gaze upon the Son and know that in the name of Christ,
  we are forgiven!

Passing the Peace of Christ

As forgiven children of God, let us share together the peace of Christ's love in our lives.

Words of Preparation (Philippians 2)

As we hear the word, let our minds be of one mind in Christ Jesus. Let us empty ourselves, and with humility and grace listen for the word of God as the Spirit speaks to us this day.

THANKSGIVING AND COMMUNION

Invitation to the Offering (Mark 14)

Remembering Mary of Bethany, we come now to pour out our gifts to God. May we remember that the poor are with us still, that our kindness and generosity are needed, even now. May we remember Christ in each face of need, in each cry for help, in each yearning for grace. May we offer our alabaster jars, the gift of our very selves. May we open ourselves and pour out the gifts of the Holy Spirit, living with us, that our gifts may flow with blessing and joy to a world in need.

SENDING FORTH

Benediction (Mark 15)

Christ is going before us, even now,
    on the road to the cross.
Christ goes before us as the way,
    the truth, and the life.
Let us feel the light of his love,
    even as we enter the darkness
        of this Holy Week.

CONTEMPORARY OPTIONS

Contemporary Gathering Words (Mark 11, Psalm 118)

Give thanks to the Lord.
    Hosanna in the highest!
For God is good.
    Hosanna in the highest!
Christ's steadfast love remains forever.
    Hosanna in the highest!
Blessed is the one who comes in the name of the Lord.
    Hosanna in the highest!

Praise Sentences (Psalm 118)

This is the day!
    This is the day!
That the Lord has made!
    That the Lord has made!
Let us rejoice!
    Let us rejoice!
And be glad in it!
    And be glad in it!

APRIL 9, 2009

Holy Thursday

B. J. Beu

COLOR

Purple

SCRIPTURE READINGS

Exodus 12:1-4 (5-10) 11-14; Psalm 116:1-4, 12-19; 1 Corinthians 11:23-26; John 13:1-17, 31b-35

THEME IDEAS

Holy Thursday, also known as Maundy Thursday, recalls Christ's celebration of the Passover feast with his disciples on the night before he was crucified. The Passover feast itself recalls the mercy of God when God passed over the homes of the Hebrew people in Egypt, sparing them from the death of every firstborn in the land. On Holy Thursday, Christ reimages this traditional Passover meal, replacing the sacrificial lamb with his own life, his own body and blood—which became the church's sacrament of Holy Communion. John's account of Holy Thursday includes Christ washing the feet of his disciples. By washing their feet, Christ shows us that we are all called to servant ministry. Finally, Christ leaves his disciples with a final commandment: to love one another, for they will be known for their love of one another.

INVITATION AND GATHERING

Call to Worship (Psalm 116)

Snares of death surround us.
Call on the name of the Lord and be saved.
The Lord is the cup of our salvation!
Pangs of suffering and grief enfold us.
Call on the name of the Lord and be saved.
The Lord is the cup of our salvation!
Bonds of distress and anguish bind us.
Call on the name of the Lord and be saved.
The Lord is the cup of our salvation!

Opening Prayer (Exodus 12)

Eternal God,
 when your people cried out in Egypt,
  you harkened to their cry;
 when your people suffered abuse and oppression,
  you harkened to their cry;
 when your people were helpless and voiceless,
  you harkened to their cry;
 when Pharaoh refused to let your people go,
  you spared their firstborn,
   that they should not suffer death
    for the sins of others;
Let your wrath pass over the righteous once more,
 as it did in Egypt long ago,
  that we may truly live
   as people redeemed by your love. Amen.

PROCLAMATION AND RESPONSE

Prayer of Confession (John 13)

Merciful God,
 when we seek to escape the chains
  of selfishness and indifference that bind us,
   hasten to our aid;
 when we turn away

from those who suffer persecution and injustice,
    heal our shut-up hearts;
when we turn a blind eye to the hungry and naked,
    the sick and imprisoned,
    the lost and the brokenhearted,
      be our vision, O God.
We ask this in the name of your Son,
    who enlivens us with the bread of heaven
    and the cup of blessing. Amen.

Words of Assurance (Psalm 116)

The Lord, who hears our voice and supplications,
    offers forgiveness of sins and fullness of grace.
Praise the Lord who is the author of our salvation!

Response to the Word (John 13)

Eternal Christ,
    help us keep your commandment
      to love one another,
      that through our love, the world may know
        that we are your disciples;
    and through our service,
      the world may be made whole
      in your holy name. Amen.

THANKSGIVING AND COMMUNION

Invitation to the Offering (John 13)

Let us bring our offerings to the one who feeds us with
the bread of life and the cup of salvation. Let us return
thanks to the one who washes our feet and brings us into
full fellowship with God. Let us offer ourselves, that we
may fulfill the law of love.

Invitation to Communion (1 Corinthians 11)

Come! Partake of the bread of heaven.
    Taste and see that the Lord is good.
Come! Draw life from the cup of blessing.
    Taste and see that the Lord is good.

Come! Enjoy a foretaste of God's heavenly banquet.
Taste and see that the Lord is good.

SENDING FORTH

Benediction

We are washed clean by the one who bathes our feet
with the waters of eternal life.
Christ has washed us clean.
We are blessed by the one who feeds our spirits
with the bread of heaven.
Christ has blessed us.
We are loved by the one who revives our souls
with the cup of salvation.
Christ has sealed us in his love.

CONTEMPORARY OPTIONS

Contemporary Gathering Words (John 13)

Don't be shy. Come and serve one another,
as Jesus has served us.
They will know we are Christians by our love!
Don't be afraid. Come and love one another,
as Jesus has loved us.
They will know we are Christians by our love!
Don't miss out. Come and wash one another with love,
as Jesus has washed us with his love.
They will know we are Christians by our love!

Praise Sentences (John 13)

Jesus feeds us with the bread of heaven.
We worship the God of Love!
Jesus nourishes us with the cup of salvation.
We worship the God of Love!
Jesus washes us clean with his love.
We worship the God of Love!

APRIL 10, 2009

Good Friday/ A Service of Tenebrae
Mary J. Scifres

COLOR
Black or None

SCRIPTURE READINGS
Isaiah 52:13–53:12; Psalm 22; Hebrews 10:16-25; John 18:1–19:42

THEME IDEAS
Lament and despair are tempered with God's promised presence throughout today's readings. Even as Isaiah reflects on the Suffering Servant, he reminds us of the gift of salvation we find in the one who loved us enough to walk humbly in righteousness and truth, even to his own death. As the psalmist cries out in despair, the same songwriter calls us to praise God and proclaim deliverance from all that would destroy us. Even as we lament Jesus' death, we are preparing to proclaim Christ's resurrection. God is with us through each step of this journey.

INVITATION AND GATHERING

Call to Worship (Hebrews 10)
Come to the sanctuary of God.
In confidence and trust, we enter this holy place.
Know that Christ has opened these doors for us.

> **By the new and living way of Christ's grace,**
> **we come to worship our God.**

Opening Prayer (Psalm 22)

> Merciful God,
> > we cry out to you,
> > > for you are holy.
> Come quickly to hear our prayer.
> Stand in the midst of our congregation,
> > that we may know your presence.
> Show us your promised salvation,
> > even on this day
> > > when hope seems to die
> > > > and despair seems to rule.

PROCLAMATION AND RESPONSE

Call to Confession (Hebrews 10)

> Without wavering, hold fast to the promise of hope. In faith and trust, let us bring our confessions before God.

Prayer of Confession (Isaiah 53)

> We, like sheep, have gone astray:
> > we have turned to our own way,
> > we have denied your presence,
> > we have betrayed your truth,
> > we have laid our iniquities upon you.
> Forgive us,
> > and guide us back
> > > into your holy presence.
> As forgiven followers,
> > may we be made new in your grace.
> As sheep of your pastures,
> > may our lives exalt you
> > > for all the world to see!
> In faith and trust, we pray. Amen.

Words of Assurance (Isaiah 53)

> Surely Christ has borne our infirmities
> > and carried our diseases.

By his bruises, we are healed.
By his love, we are made whole.

THANKSGIVING AND COMMUNION

Invitation to the Offering (Psalm 22, John 18–19)

Let us pour ourselves out like water. Let us give ourselves
fully to the one who has given his very life, that all may
know the love of God.

Prayer of Thanksgiving (Psalm 22)

God of unending generosity,
  we praise you this day.
We cry out with gratitude
  for the many gifts you have given us,
  but most especially
    for your gift of life on this earth.
May the life and teachings of your Son Jesus live in us:
  that the hungry might eat and be satisfied,
  that the thirsty might drink and be revived,
  that the poor might receive generosity and kindness.
With humble thankfulness, we pray. Amen.

SENDING FORTH

Benediction (John 19)

Christ has died.
  The tomb is sealed.
It is finished.

CONTEMPORARY OPTIONS

Contemporary Gathering Words

On this day strangely called "good,"
  we are challenged to find goodness,
    even in the face of evil.
May the goodness of Christ's unending love
  bring us hope that never wavers.
May the presence of Christ in our lives

bring forth goodness and love in one another.
May this time of gathering
strengthen our faith in God
and our trust in this body of Christ.

Praise Sentences (Psalm 22)
Praise God to the ends of the earth.
Proclaim Christ's deliverance to all.
Praise God to the ends of the earth.
Proclaim Christ's deliverance to all.

APRIL 12, 2009

Easter Sunday

Edward W. Paup

COLOR

White

EASTER READINGS

Acts 10:34-43; Psalm 118:1-2, 14-24; 1 Corinthians 15:1-11;
John 20:1-18 or Mark 16:1-8

THEME IDEAS

Resurrection—light and life—comes from the creative energy of God who makes all things new. This holy feast day is the core of the Christian faith. It celebrates God's activity in the risen Christ on the first day of the new creation. God's response to the darkness of the crucifixion parallels God's response to the darkness shrouding the earth on the first day of creation—"Let there be light." Darkness and death are not the final words. They are light and life. The liturgies of Easter connect us with the presence of the risen Christ who calls us to be heralds of this good news today.

INVITATION AND GATHERING

Call to Worship (Acts 10)

God sent Jesus to preach peace, saying,
God is God of all.
We gather to worship as witnesses.

God anointed Jesus with the Holy Spirit,
with the power to heal and do good.
We gather to worship as witnesses.
They put Jesus to death,
but God raised him on the third day.
We gather to worship as witnesses.
We are called to preach peace, saying,
God is God of all.
We gather to worship as witnesses.

—Or—

Call to Worship (John 20)

We run to the tomb
to be forever surprised.
Christ is risen!
Through our tears of sorrow and despair,
we don't recognize him.
Christ is risen!
Then he calls us by name.
Christ is risen!
We run into the world announcing,
"We have seen the Lord!"
Christ is risen!

Opening Prayer or Prayer of Thanksgiving (Acts 10)

O God,
we thank you for sending Jesus
to proclaim your peace,
and that you are God of all.
We give you thanks
that the forces of evil
could destroy neither him
nor your peace.
We gather to worship you
and to proclaim
that we are your Easter people.
By your Holy Spirit
help us preach your peace

by the way we live,
in the name of the risen Christ. Amen.

PROCLAMATION AND RESPONSE

Prayer of Confession or Response to the Word (John 20)
O God,
>we love surprises,
>>but this is the greatest of all.
Jesus Christ is risen.
He is risen indeed!
Just when we give in
>to the forces of darkness and death,
>>there you come again
>>>and roll away the stone.
Surprise!
O God,
>help us offer your wonderful surprises
>>to all of your creation,
>>>in the name of the risen one. Amen.

Words of Assurance (John 20, Easter)
Surprise! The stone is rolled away!
Christ is risen! Be gone, darkness and death!
You have no power here! Christ is risen!
Christ is risen indeed!

Passing the Peace of Christ (Easter)
Christ is risen! Share this great news with one another as we offer signs of joy and love by passing the peace of Christ.

Response to the Word or Opening Prayer (John 20, Mark 16)
O God,
>we worship on this holy day,
>>knowing that we are your Easter people.
We read the story again
>and marvel at the sight of the rising Son.

It's as if we were a polar people
who wonder at the glimpse
of the light of the sun
after a season of darkness.
Memory recalls the return of light,
yet we still marvel and wonder
at its arrival.
Help us reflect the light of your rising Son,
that others might see and give glory to you,
by the power of your Holy Spirit. Amen.

THANKSGIVING AND COMMUNION

Invitation to the Offering (Psalm 118)

Give thanks to God.
God's steadfast love endures forever.
God is our strength and our salvation.
God's steadfast love endures forever.
God does not give us over to death, but to life.
God's steadfast love endures forever.
The stone that the builders rejected has become
the chief cornerstone.
God's steadfast love endures forever.
Sharing our gratitude, let us offer signs of God's love
in the giving of our tithes and our offerings.

Offering Prayer (Psalm 118)

God of light and life,
we give you thanks and praise
this Easter day.
Your steadfast love calls to us
with its power to overcome
death and darkness.
Our joy overflows this day.
May our gifts overflow
with this same joy,
that others may see your light
and know new life through your risen Son,

Jesus the Christ. Amen.
(Mary J. Scifres)

SENDING FORTH

Benediction (Acts 10)
May the risen Christ go with us—
  before us to show us the way;
  behind us to encourage us;
  beside us to befriend us;
  above us to watch over us;
  and live within us and through us,
    that all might know the peace of God.

CONTEMPORARY OPTIONS

Contemporary Gathering Words (John 20)
It's Easter. What shall we say about it?
  God is the source of light and life.
But there's so much darkness and death in the world.
  God is the source of light and life.
May this Easter worship renew us,
that we might announce with our lives:
  God is the source of light and life.

Praise Sentences (Psalm 118)
Praise God, for God is good.
God's steadfast love endures forever.
Praise God, for God is our strength and our salvation.
This is the day that the Lord has made,
  let us rejoice and be glad in it.
Praise God!

APRIL 19, 2009

Second Sunday of Easter
Laura Jaquith Bartlett

COLOR
White

SCRIPTURE READINGS
Acts 4:32-35; Psalm 133; 1 John 1:1–2:2; John 20:19-31

THEME IDEAS
Fellowship is a term we toss around frequently in church life, but too often we simply mean chatting with friends during coffee hour. True Christian fellowship is a radical concept, as the communal life outlined in Acts illustrates. Notice that the power of the community lies in the willingness of its members to testify to Christ's resurrection. In the gospel reading, the disciples are gathered together, but their focus is fear and doubt. Only when *each* one (including Thomas) is willing to testify to the resurrection is the stage set for the "great grace" that flows so freely in the Acts story—the story of a community gathered in one heart and soul.

INVITATION AND GATHERING

Call to Worship (Easter, Acts 4)
We gather in the name of the risen Lord.
Christ is risen! Alleluia!

We gather as sisters and brothers of the resurrected one.
Christ is risen! Alleluia!
We gather to share our faith and to worship God.
Christ is risen! Alleluia!
We gather to proclaim the good news of Easter!
Christ is risen! Alleluia!

Opening Prayer (Easter, Acts 4)

God of the resurrection,
we gather this morning
as a community of believers.
We come with joy to greet one another
and to tell again and again the amazing news:
Christ is risen!
Love is victorious over death!
You have given us new life
in the name of your Son!
May our singing, praying, listening, and proclaiming
be a testimony to the power of your love
to make us a new creation
as a community of faith.
We pray in the name of the risen Christ. Amen.

PROCLAMATION AND RESPONSE

Prayer of Confession

God of mercy,
we come celebrating our unity,
but we confess the many ways
that we are divided.
Our nationality, ethnic origin, economic status,
gender, age, and musical preferences
all too often obscure the common calling
we share in Christ's name.
May our common identity as your children
and our communal witness to Christ
bind us together in your name.

Forgive our tendency toward separation and division,
and remind us that we are your Easter people.

Words of Assurance (1 John 1–2)

When we walk in the light of Christ,
we have fellowship with one another.
When we confess our sins,
the One who is faithful and just forgives our sins
and cleanses us from all unrighteousness.
For in the death and resurrection of Jesus Christ,
God has showered mercy upon the entire world. Amen.

Passing the Peace of Christ (Psalm 133)

Teach the refrain (by rote) to "O Look and Wonder (¡Miren Qué Bueno!)" and instruct the congregation to move about to pass the peace as they sing. While a soloist or small group sings the stanzas, people greet one another, then move about while singing the refrain. Continue for several minutes. Have a few people prepared ahead of time to model this.

Invitation to the Word

Dear God,
as we hear your word,
may we be transformed
into a true community of believers,
ready to go into the world
to testify that Christ is alive
and active in our lives today. Amen.

Response to the Word

In view of scripture's emphasis on testimony and faith, a unison reading of a church creed or statement of faith would be an appropriate response to the word.

THANKSGIVING AND COMMUNION

Invitation to the Offering

All that we have belongs to God. As we celebrate our unity as a community of faith and focus our hearts on the risen Christ, we joyfully lay our possessions at the altar

[Lord's table]. Through the grace of God and the bounty of this church, we have the ability to share our gifts so that all may have what they need to live. We thank God for the opportunity to truly be in fellowship with one another and with the world through our offerings today.

Offering Prayer

Generous and surprising God,
> when we thought that death
>> had claimed your only Son,
>>> you amazed us with the resurrection.
Surprise us again
> with your ability to turn these humble offerings
>> into gifts that will transform the world
>>> through our witness to your love.
We lay our very lives at your feet, O God,
> knowing that you will use us
>> to proclaim and embody the gospel. Amen.

SENDING FORTH

Benediction

Go now with the love of God, the grace of Jesus Christ,
and the fellowship of the Holy Spirit.
> **Christ is risen! Alleluia!**
Go to share your faith and your lives.
> **Christ is risen! Alleluia!**
Go to proclaim the good news of Easter.
> **Christ is risen! Alleluia!**

CONTEMPORARY OPTIONS

Contemporary Gathering Words (John 20:29)

We are people of the twenty-first century,
far removed from the upper room.
> **"Blessed are those who have not seen**
> **and yet have come to believe."**
We have put away the festive trumpets,
the fancy clothes, the chocolate bunnies of Easter Sunday.

Must the message of Easter be put away for another year?
**"Blessed are those who have not seen
and yet have come to believe."**
We still seek the One who offers victory over death,
whose love conquers evil.
**"Blessed are those who have not seen
and yet have come to believe."**
We gather to worship the risen Christ,
who offers us new life.
**"Blessed are those who have not seen
and yet have come to believe."**

Praise Sentences (Psalm 133)

How very good and pleasant it is
when we all live together in unity!
It is like precious oil on the head,
running down upon the beard.
It is like young children
sitting side-by-side with seniors in worship.
It is like corporate executives
picking in the fields next to farmhands.
It is like Jews, Christians, and Muslims
living in peace in Jerusalem.
How very good and pleasant it is
when we all live together in unity!

APRIL 26, 2009

Third Sunday of Easter

Mary J. Scifres

COLOR

White

SCRIPTURE READINGS

Acts 3:12-19; Psalm 4; 1 John 3:1-7; Luke 24:36b-48

THEME IDEAS

Beloved, we are the children of God. Even in our joy and disbelief, Christ is with us. Even in our sinfulness, God's forgiveness is ours in Christ's name. Even in our humanity, we are called to be Christlike, righteous and loving. These are not easy lessons, and yet, they are the lessons proclaimed in 1 John and Luke 24. Bringing these lessons to life, that these lessons might be our lives, is the task before us.

INVITATION AND GATHERING

Call to Worship (1 John 3, Luke 24)
Peace be with you.
And also with you.
Come and see the love God has given to us.
Come and see what it means to be children of God.
Come with this hope, that Christ's presence is real.
With joy, we come to see the Lord.

Opening Prayer (Luke 24)

Miraculous God,
> come to us now,
> even as your Son came
>> to those first disciples
>>> on the shores of Galilee.

Speak your peace to our hearts.
Touch us with your Holy Spirit.
Reveal your word,
> that we may hear your message this day,
> and live as your disciples
>> in the days and years to come.

In Christ's name, we pray. Amen.

PROCLAMATION AND RESPONSE

Prayer of Confession (1 John 3, Luke 24)

Holy and righteous one,
> we are stunned by the miracles
>> of new life and forgiveness you offer.

When our awe turns to disbelief,
> renew us with your joy.

When our fear turns to rejection,
> lead us into your presence.

When our stumbling leads to sin,
> forgive us by your grace,
> and direct our steps
>> in your paths of righteousness.

In Christ's name, we pray. Amen.

Words of Assurance and Passing the Peace of Christ (1 John 3)

Beloved, we are God's children now.
Because we have this hope,
> we are forgiven and purified.

As beloved children,
> we are made one with Christ
>> and brought into the righteousness of God.

Let us share this hope and love with one another
as we greet one another
in the name of the risen Christ.

Words of Preparation (Luke 24)

Even as the risen Christ appeared to those first disciples,
so Christ is present with us now. Let us pray for open
minds and ready hearts to hear and receive the word of
God.

Prayer of Preparation (1 John 3, Luke 24)

Risen Christ,
come to us now.
Open our ears,
that we may hear your word.
Open our minds,
that we may understand
the scriptures before us.
Speak to our hearts,
that our lives may be transformed
by your love.
Guide our steps as we go forth,
that we may be your beloved children,
witnessing to your resurrection,
and proclaiming your message
throughout the earth. Amen.

THANKSGIVING AND COMMUNION

Invitation to the Offering (Luke 24:41)

"Have you anything here to eat?" Jesus asks. Have we
anything here to share? As the ushers wait upon us, may
we share our gifts, that others may be fed.

Offering Prayer (Luke 24)

Author of life and Giver of all gifts,
we thank you for the many blessings of our lives.
Receive now these gifts
and transform them

with the power of your love.
May they become witnesses to your resurrection,
    proclaiming your power and forgiveness
        in our community and throughout the world.

SENDING FORTH

Benediction (Psalm 4, Luke 24)
May the light of God's face shine upon us.
May the beauty of Christ's love shine through us.
May the power of God's Spirit flow within us.
**May we go forth as God's beloved children,
revealing the risen Christ in all that we say,
and in all that we do.**

CONTEMPORARY OPTIONS

Contemporary Gathering Words (Luke 24)
Why are you frightened?
Why do doubts arise in your hearts
    and haunt your steps?
Christ is here.
Even now, the risen Christ is among us!

Praise Sentences (1 John 3)
See what love God has given to us!
We are all God's children now!

MAY 3, 2009

Fourth Sunday of Easter

B. J. Beu

COLOR
White

SCRIPTURE READINGS
Acts 4:5-12; Psalm 23; 1 John 3:16-24; John 10:11-18

THEME IDEAS
The good shepherd and the shepherding love of Christ focus today's readings. While Acts focuses on the unique saving ability of Jesus Christ, John implies that other sheep are part of God's fold. The familiar words of Psalm 23 become fresh when interwoven with the words of John 10 and 1 John 3. Though not in today's readings, conjoining Psalm 23 with Isaiah 40:31 provides a vision of strength and comfort.

INVITATION AND GATHERING

Call to Worship or Litany (Isaiah 40:31, Psalm 23)
Those who wait for the Lord shall renew their strength.
The Lord is my shepherd, I shall not want.
He makes me lie down in green pastures.
He leads me beside the still waters.
They shall mount up with wings like eagles.
He restores my soul.

**He leads me in the paths of righteousness
for his name's sake.**
They shall run and not be weary.
**Yea though I walk through the valley
of the shadow of death I shall fear no evil,
for thou art with me.**
They shall walk and not faint.
**Surely goodness and mercy shall follow me
all the days of my life, and I shall dwell in the house
of the Lord forever.**

Opening Prayer (Psalm 23)
Shepherding God,
    you bring us into your presence
        and shower us with your love.
You lead us beside the still waters
    and restore our souls.
Touch our hearts and minds,
    that we may live your love
        and abide in your grace. Amen.

PROCLAMATION AND RESPONSE

Prayer of Confession (John 10, 1 John 3)
God of many pastures,
    we never tire of hearing
        the voice of our shepherd;
    we never tire of hearing
        the call to lay our burdens down;
    we never tire of hearing
        the invitation to dwell in your house forever.
Forgive us, loving shepherd,
    when we try to keep you as our own—
        thinking that we alone have your love,
        thinking that others wander alone
            without your care and guidance.
Open our eyes,
    that we may recognize the sheep of your fold

wherever they may be
and whatever they may look like. Amen.

Words of Assurance (Psalm 23)

The one who lays his life down for the sheep
will surely rescue us and lead us to safe pastures.
Through the love and grace of our shepherd,
goodness and mercy shall follow us
all the days of our lives,
and we shall dwell securely forever.

Response to the Word (1 John 3)

Eternal God, our guide and guardian,
you call us to abide in your love
and walk in your grace.
Help us live your love
not only in our words
but also in our deeds.
Enlighten our minds to your teachings,
that we may be servants of your love.
Transform our church,
that we may be shepherds
of your grace. Amen.

Call to Prayer (Psalm 23)

Come, all who are weary and need rest. Come, all who
thirst for the springs that well up to eternal life. Come, all
who hunger and thirst for righteousness. Lift up your
prayers to our shepherd—the one who leads us through
the shadow of death, the one who leads us into life.

THANKSGIVING AND COMMUNION

Invitation to the Offering (John 10, 1 John 3)

The good shepherd calls us to love one another.
We come, abiding in love.
The shepherd of love calls us to give of ourselves.
We come, abiding in faith.
The shepherd of life calls us to be a blessing to others.
We come, abiding in God's blessings.

SENDING FORTH

Benediction (1 John 3)
Go forth in God's care,
taking love wherever you go.
We will abide in God's love.
Go forth in God's name,
taking Christ wherever you go.
We will abide in God's love.
Go forth in God's grace,
sharing mercy with everyone you meet.
We will abide in God's love.

CONTEMPORARY OPTIONS

Contemporary Gathering Words (Acts 4, John 10)
Who is the cornerstone of our faith?
Jesus is our cornerstone!
Who is our shepherd in these dark days?
Jesus is our shepherd!
Who can save us from this world of pain?
Jesus is our savior!

Praise Sentences (Psalm 23)
The Lord is our shepherd, we shall not want.
Praise God, our Lord, and our life!
The Lord is our shepherd; we lie down in peace.
Praise God, our Lord, and our life!

MAY 10, 2009

Fifth Sunday of Easter/Festival of the Christian Home/Mother's Day

Joanne Carlson Brown

COLOR
White

SCRIPTURE READINGS
Acts 8:26-40; Psalm 22:25-31; 1 John 4:7-21; John 15:1-8

THEME IDEAS
Proclaiming and living the good news is at the heart of these passages—the good news of the transforming love of God for all people. Our only authentic response to such love is to love God and God's people in return. It is love in action—a love that bears fruit; a love that reaches out across boundaries of race, class, and sex; a love that forms us all into one family of God; a love that ushers in the kingdom of God.

INVITATION AND GATHERING

Call to Worship (Psalm 22, 1 John 4, Acts 8)
Beloved, we are gathered together
to praise the God of transforming love.
    From the ends of the earth,
    we remember and turn to God.
As the family of God, we reach out

and invite all to join us on our journey.
Hand in hand, and heart to heart,
we have come to worship God,
and to proclaim our faith to all the world.

Opening Prayer (Psalm 22, 1 John 4, Acts 8, John 15)

Ever-loving and transforming God,
we come this morning
with praise and thanksgiving.
We come as part of your family—
a family that binds us together
across time and space,
across the barriers of race,
class, and sex.
May this time of worship empower us
to embody your good news.
May we always abide in you,
and you in us.
May we be immersed
in the water of your word
and promises and love.
May we be so filled with your Spirit
that we can't help but proclaim to all
your goodness as our God. Amen.

PROCLAMATION AND RESPONSE

Prayer of Confession

Ever present God,
your love is poured out on all peoples.
We have been slow to receive it for ourselves.
We have been reluctant to acknowledge
the extension of your love
to people who are different from us.
We have been slow to live out your love—
our actions have not matched our words;
our heart has not matched your message.
Help us hear your call

and feel your transformative power,
   that we can truly be the family of God,
      embracing all your children.
May your Spirit fill us with courage
   to proclaim the good news
      of your all-encompassing love.
Strengthen our resolve and guide our actions,
   that we may truly bear good fruit.

Words of Assurance (1 John 4, John 15)

Beloved, God is love and God loves us
   with a mother's fierce tenderness.
If we abide in this love,
   God will hear and respond in loving forgiveness,
      so that we may bear the fruit
         of love and compassion and justice.

Passing the Peace of Christ (1 John 4)

Beloved, let us love one another because love is from God.
Let us greet one another in love, the love that binds us together as the family of God.

Response to the Word (Acts 8, John 15)

All-empowering God,
   help us respond to your word
      and your promises and your love
         with the faithfulness of the Ethiopian eunuch.
May your word abide in us;
   and may we abide in you.

THANKSGIVING AND COMMUNION

Invitation to the Offering (1 John 4, Acts 8, John 15)

We have received the greatest gift of all—God's transforming love. And we are called to extend that gift to all
the world. We do this through our words and our actions.
Our offering is a visible sign of our gratitude for what we
have received; it is a way of bearing fruit, of showing our
love. Let us respond to God's bountiful love with generous gifts of love.

Offering Prayer (1 John 4, Acts 8)

We give thanks that we are part of your family, O God.
We offer these gifts of tangible love,
    that they may be used
        to proclaim the good news to all,
        especially those who feel alone and unloved. Amen.

SENDING FORTH

Benediction (Acts 8, 1 John 4, John 15)

Go forth, abiding in God's love.
Go forth, claiming your identity
    as beloved children of God.
Go forth, to share the good news
    with all you meet.

CONTEMPORARY OPTIONS

Contemporary Gathering Words (Acts 8, 1 John 4, John 15, Psalm 22)

Come, family of God.
Come worship the God of amazing love.
Come praise the God of all the families of the earth.
Come and abide in the God of extravagant welcome.

Praise Sentences (Psalm 22)

Praise God, all who see God!
Praise God, all who burn with the fire of God's Spirit!
Praise God, all who remember God's promises!
Worship God, all who belong to God's family!

MAY 17, 2009

Sixth Sunday of Easter
Linda K. Crowe

COLOR
White

SCRIPTURE READINGS
Acts 10:44-48; Psalm 98; 1 John 5:1-6; John 15:9-17

THEME IDEAS
The underlying theme woven through these lections is love—a love that is active rather than passive. Psalm 98 is an enthusiastic invitation to celebrate God's love and faithfulness. 1 John 5 offers a connection between God's love for us and our love for others. John 15 provides an explicit call to loving faithfulness, a call to service in Jesus' name. Jesus proclaims, "Love one another as I have loved you" (John 15:12). The commandment to love is a call to action and service, not a call to quiet contemplation.

INVITATION AND GATHERING

Call to Worship (Psalm 98)
With hearts full of joy, let us give thanks
for God's steadfast love and faithfulness!
   O sing to God a new song!
With songs and celebration,
let us bring God our thanks and praise!

O sing to God a new song!
With a joyful noise, let us worship God!
O sing to God a new song!

Opening Prayer (Psalm 98, John 15)
Faithful, loving God,
    be with us now.
We have gathered
    to bring you our thanks and praise.
We have come
    to learn your ways of love.
You have called us
    to keep your commandments
    and to love as you love.
You have chosen us
    to bear fruit in your holy name.
Faithful, loving God,
    help us remember
      that our words and actions
        matter in this world.
Guide us to witness to your ways.
Lead us to be instruments of your love.
With all that we say and do,
    may our lives resound
      with songs of joy to you! Amen.

PROCLAMATION AND RESPONSE

Prayer of Confession (John 15, Acts 10)
Gracious and faithful God,
    hear us now.
We seek to follow you.
We strive to serve you.
We want to be filled
    with your Holy Spirit.
In spite of our longing,
    we stumble and struggle.
We do things we should not do,

and we fail to do
    the things we should.
We harm ourselves and others
    and your good creation.
Most of all,
    in our failings,
        we hurt you.
Forgive us, God.
Grant us strength and courage
    to be the people you would have us be.
Fill us with your Spirit
    and abide in us.
Let our lives bear witness
    to your steadfast love and faithfulness,
        in Jesus' name.

Words of Assurance

Let us begin anew to be the people God calls us to be:
    instruments of God's love in this world.
By the grace and love of God, we are forgiven!
Thanks be to God!

Invitation to the Word

Open our minds and hearts, O God,
    to receive the wisdom and blessings
        offered now.
In these moments,
    guide our hearing and our understanding.
In the days to come,
    guide our witness to your holy word. Amen.

THANKSGIVING AND COMMUNION

Invitation to the Offering (John 15)

Our financial gifts enable us to do God's work in this world. Our offerings enable us to love and bless our neighbors, both near and far away. Financial gifts reflect faith and commitment. As God has blessed us so generously, let us be generous with God!

Offering Prayer (John 15)

Gracious and generous God,
  you call us to love one another
    as you love us.
May our gifts reveal our love for you.
May our lives be reflections of your love
  as we share with a world in need.
We ask for your blessing
  on these gifts and on our lives.
We pray in Jesus' name. Amen.

Communion Prayer of Thanksgiving (John 15)

We give you thanks, gracious God,
  that you have welcomed us to this table.
Here we touch and taste and hear again
  the signs of your love for us.
We thank you for the blessing
  of Christ's presence in this holy meal.
By the power of your Holy Spirit,
  go with us now into the world,
    to proclaim the good news of your love,
    and to love and bless one another.
We pray in the name of Jesus Christ. Amen.

SENDING FORTH

Benediction (John 15, 1 John 5)

Go now into the world.
Love God, and obey God's commandments.
  We go forth in love.
Abide in God's love.
For in God's love, your joy will be complete!
  We go forth in love.

CONTEMPORARY OPTIONS

Contemporary Gathering Words (Psalm 98)

Sing to God a new song!
  Sing to God, for God has done marvelous things!

Celebrate God's steadfast love and faithfulness!
Sing to God, for God has done marvelous things!
With praise and thanksgiving and joyful noise,
come into the presence of God!
Sing to God, for God has done marvelous things!

Praise Sentences (Psalm 98)
Shout for joy, all the earth!
Sing praise to God!
Celebrate God's steadfast love!
Sing praise to God!
Sing of God's faithfulness!
Sing praise to God!

MAY 24, 2009

Ascension Sunday
Bryan Schneider-Thomas

COLOR
White

SCRIPTURE READINGS
Acts 1:1-11; Psalm 47; Ephesians 1:15-23; Luke 24:44-53

THEME IDEAS
Power is a dominant theme in today's readings: the power of the risen Christ who is glorified and the promised power of the Holy Spirit. These texts invite us to reflect upon how these two powers work together in our life of faith. They also anticipate the conclusion of the Easter season next Sunday on Pentecost. Today we celebrate the power of Jesus Christ, while also yearning for the gift of power in the Holy Spirit.

INVITATION AND GATHERING

Call to Worship (Luke 24)
Come gather 'round; Jesus is here.
We wait for the coming Spirit.
Come gather 'round; see the power of Christ before you.
With joy, we praise God.

Opening Prayer (Ephesians 1)
Almighty God,
through Jesus Christ,

you revealed to us a power
that has no parallel.
May the eyes of our heart
be enlightened to this power
and all it has done in our lives.
Pour out your Spirit of power upon us,
that we may proclaim your glory
and your grace. Amen.

PROCLAMATION AND RESPONSE

Prayer of Confession

Lord Jesus Christ, in you we see awesome power.
You triumph over death and bring forth new life.
You stand over all earthly powers.
You are the head of the church.
Yet, we often fail to acknowledge this power in our lives.
We see violence in the world.
We see injustice in our communities.
We see hunger and need among our neighbors.
We see longing for something more.
We see failures and faults in our lives.
In all these things, we feel powerless.
Forgive our hesitance to call upon you.
Forgive our propensity to rely upon ourselves.
Forgive our reluctance to acknowledge your power.
Speak your words of power again.
May your will may be done on earth as it is in heaven.
Amen.

Words of Assurance (Ephesians 1)

May God give you a spirit of wisdom and revelation,
that the power of Jesus Christ may be visible in your life.
By the grace of Jesus Christ we are forgiven
and empowered to serve.

Passing the Peace of Christ

God's power is a glorious inheritance among the saints.
It is a power manifested in love, forgiveness, and peace.

May the power of peace be with you today.
And also with you.
Let us pass the peace of Christ.

Response to the Word (Ephesians 1, Luke 24)
In these words, we hear of the power of Christ
and the promise of a Spirit of power.
We hear the ancient story come alive in our lives.
We seek a spirit of wisdom and revelation in Christ.
We await a spirit of power from God.
Come, Lord Jesus. Come, Holy Spirit.
Come into our lives.

THANKSGIVING AND COMMUNION

Invitation to the Offering or Invitation to Communion
Come to the table of peace.
Come to the table of love.
Come to the table of joy.
Come to the table of power.
Come to the table of Christ.

Great Thanksgiving
*(The following prayer may replace the preface and conclusion
of the Great Thanksgiving, or it may be used by itself at an appropriate time in the service.)*
You are worthy of all our praise, O God,
for you are the source of all good power.
By your power,
heaven and earth were formed.
By your power,
you created us and gave us life.
By your power,
we are guided and protected.
By your power,
Jesus Christ triumphed over the grave.
By your power,
the Holy Spirit comes to sustain and care for us.

And so, in praise and gratitude, we join the generations
of the faithful in singing your praise.
*(If desired, continue with the traditional Great Thanksgiving,
beginning with the Sanctus)*
When Jesus ascended into heaven, he promised
his followers a baptism with the Holy Spirit,
a power from on high. Clothe us in this Spirit,
that we might share a common ministry
of service to the world.
By your power,
   fill our voices with stories of your grace.
By your power,
   strengthen our hands for the work of your mercy.
By your power,
   transform us into your representatives of your love.
In great joy and anticipation, empowered by your Spirit,
we await the return of Christ, as we offer praise to you,
   Almighty God, in whom we live and move
and have our being.
   Amen.

SENDING FORTH

Benediction
   In the presence of Christ, we have gathered.
      In the grace of Christ, we depart.
   May God clothe you with power on high.
      May God put this power to work in each of us.

CONTEMPORARY OPTIONS

Contemporary Gathering Words
   Power!
      Power!
   Power on high is given to you.
      Power that enlightens.
   Power that sustains.
      Power to give praise to God.
      Power!

Praise Sentences (Psalm 47)
Clap your hands.
Shout for joy.
Sing out praise.
Exalt the God of power!

MAY 31, 2009

Pentecost Sunday
Sara Dunning Lambert

COLOR
Red

SCRIPTURE READINGS
Acts 2:1-21; Romans 8:22-27; John 15:26-27; 16:4b-15; Psalm 104:24-34, 35b

THEME IDEAS
The feast of Pentecost is celebrated today with images of rushing wind, tongues of flame, and with the breaking down of language barriers to receive the message of the gospel through the power of the Holy Spirit. The Romans passage uses the metaphor of birth to describe the infant church awaiting guidance of the Spirit, while making the transition from old ways to a new life in Christ. John introduces the Advocate, or Spirit of Truth, as the guide for those who follow Christ. The psalm proclaims that all creation rejoices at the touch of God's hand. At Pentecost, the mission of the church is to reach out to the world with the love of Christ.

INVITATION AND GATHERING

Call to Worship (Acts 2, John 15–16)
With tongues of flame, the Holy Spirit descends
to burn in our hearts anew.

Unite us, Holy Spirit!
Like the rush of wind, we sense God's presence
blowing afresh throughout the world.
Unite us, Holy Spirit!
Across the barriers of language and culture,
Christ's message of love and grace is heard.
Unite us, Holy Spirit!
Divine Advocate, we seek your guidance
as we search for the Spirit of Truth.
Unite us, Holy Spirit! Amen.

Opening Prayer (Acts 2, Romans 8)

Holy One,
    ignite within us a fiery passion
        for your mission in the world today.
Warm us by the Spirit's dancing tongues of flame,
    that we may feel your kindling blaze within,
        urging us to do your greater good.
Make us wholly present to experience a new birth,
    and awaken possibilities within us
        to share your love in the world.
In this love and abundance,
    we come to celebrate your harvest—
        a harvest bearing the first fruits of the Spirit
           within us.
Show us how to use these gifts,
    as we listen for your truth
        in the gentle breeze of your Spirit.

PROCLAMATION AND RESPONSE

Prayer of Confession (Romans 8, Acts 2)

Heavenly Father,
    you dwell within us
        in sighs too deep for words,
           yet we cannot hear you.
Caring Mother,
    you wrap us tenderly in fierce love,

you give us the breath of life,
    yet we cannot touch you.
Brother Jesus,
    we yearn for your presence,
    we seek your abundant grace,
        yet we cannot feel it.
Sister Spirit,
    you prepare to sear our souls for your purpose,
        yet we allow our somber selves to intrude,
           shutting our minds to your power.
Remind us, we pray,
    that we need only trust in the giver of life
        to find the hope and faith you have promised.
Gather us up in the winds of your favor
    and carry us to ever greater heights,
        through Christ who loves us still.

Words of Assurance (John 15–16, Acts 2)
Do not be afraid.
Our Comforter and Advocate has come.
Rejoice in the knowledge that all is forgiven.
People of the Spirit, listen.
The wind that drives the heavens—
  the wind that soars above and beyond us all,
    unifies us in God's love.
Keep the Spirit's flame alight within your heart.
Await the new birth in Christ that is promised to all.

Passing the Peace of Christ (Acts 2)
Feel the caress of the Holy Spirit in the healing breath of
hope. See the bright embers of faith beckon each of us to
unity in God. Greet one another in the assurance that the
peace of Christ is ever present.

Response to the Word (Acts 2, Romans 8, John 15–16)
Source of all,
    open us to your word.
Open our eyes to the incendiary faith of your disciples.
Open our minds to the gift of becoming first fruits

III

of the harvest.
Open our ears to hear your rushing, mighty Spirit.
Open our mouths to cry out for peace
    in a war-torn world.
Open our hands to bring justice to the downtrodden.
Open our hearts to share hope with the hopeless.
Amen.

THANKSGIVING AND COMMUNION

Invitation to the Offering (Acts 2)
Gracious God,
    as we stand in your holy place
    we feel your bright Spirit surge within us.
We are on fire with the knowledge
    that we may be your witness to the world.
Help us speak in language
    that others will understand.
Ignite within us
    a need to share the abundance of our lives.
We lay before you
    our gifts of faith, hope, and love.
We pledge to give more of our time,
    more of our hearts,
    and more of our material possessions,
        that we may serve your greater good. Amen.

Offering Prayer (Acts 2, Romans 8)
Precious Lord,
    we hunger for the light and strength
        that only the Spirit can bring.
Feed us and strengthen us,
    as we learn to feed others.
Fill us with the breath of your spirit
    as you search our hearts.
Take our lives
    as proof of our faithfulness.
Take our gifts
    as proof of our love.

Use them to your purpose
here on earth.

SENDING FORTH

Benediction (Acts 2)

May the power of the Holy Spirit
transform you with the healing fire
that unifies the world.
Let the wind of that first Pentecost
teach you of God's grace, love, hope,
and mystery.
With tongues of flame,
may you be marked for Christ.
Go out in faith and abiding love.

CONTEMPORARY OPTIONS

Contemporary Gathering Words (Acts 2)

The flame of the Spirit burns in our lives,
warming all in its path.
Holy Spirit, come!
Hear the Spirit calling out of God's holy wind,
rising up toward the sky.
Holy Spirit, come!
The intoxicating breath of hope fills us with love.
Holy Spirit, come!
God calls us to listen, feel, and follow!
Holy Spirit, come!

Praise Sentences (Acts 2)

The Holy Spirit is the fire that doesn't consume
or destroy, but energizes, warms, and excites!
The Holy Spirit is the wind that lifts us up
to heights beyond joy!
The Holy Spirit is the birth that brings us into
life with Christ, as a mother births a child!
The Holy Spirit calls us to testify to the truth!

JUNE 7, 2009

Trinity Sunday

Rebecca J. Kruger Gaudino

COLOR

White

SCRIPTURE READINGS

Isaiah 6:1-8; Psalm 29; Romans 8:12-17; John 3:1-17

THEME IDEAS

All of our texts this Sunday speak of God in mysterious and ultimate terms. They speak of the God of power and splendor who conducts cosmic business in the lofty courts of heaven, who reveals truth through the sign-doer and riddle-maker Jesus, and who moves through the elusive Spirit Wind. What mystery! Our words—yes, even our Trinitarian stammering—buckle beneath the weight of transcendence our words attempt to convey. What majesty! And yet, each text also points to places in life where ultimate and unlimited reality brushes up against, and impinges upon, our limited lives for powerful, life-changing experiences. These experiences proclaim that we—the lowly, the enslaved, the woeful—are drawn into the cosmic story line of God's immense life and intentions. Trinity Sunday is the Sunday to celebrate God as the mystery that shimmers in our lives.

INVITATION AND GATHERING

Call to Worship (Psalm 29)
(Ask the congregation to "speak up"!)
The voice of the Lord flashes flames of fire.
Ascribe to the Lord glory and strength.
The voice of the Lord shakes the wilderness!
Worship the Lord in holy splendor.
The Lord sits enthroned as sovereign forever.
In God's congregation, all say, "Glory!"

Opening Prayer (Isaiah 6, Psalm 29)
O Sovereign of the universe,
　　we stand in your temple,
　　　　proclaiming your splendor and majesty.
You are the Holy One!
You are full of glory!
You speak,
　　and the oaks whirl
　　　　and the cedars fall!
We stand in your presence
　　in awe and humility.
We stand in your presence
　　with boldness and courage.
We look and listen
　　for your presence here today. Amen.

PROCLAMATION AND RESPONSE

Prayer of Confession (Isaiah 6, John 3)
We know much about earthly things,
　　but so little about heavenly things.
We stand in your presence, O God,
　　but fail to see the hem of your robe
　　　　in our midst—
　　　　　　much less your presence,
　　　　　　　　far above, upon the throne of heaven.
We do not often see your seraphim

in flight around your throne.
We do not often hear their voices
    or feel the very foundations about us
        tremble at their loud praise.
Open our lives to your mystery,
    power, and glory.
Open our lives to you, O Holy One. Amen.

Words of Assurance (Psalm 29, John 3)
Today we will hear of heavenly things
    that can transform our lives forever.
We will hear of God's miraculous presence
    with us and among us and for us.
In God's temple, let all of us say, "Glory!"
"Glory!"

Passing the Peace of Christ (Romans 8)
Hear this mystery: we are all the children and heirs of the Holy One. Welcome your brothers and sisters with the peace that God has given us through Christ Jesus.

Response to the Word (Isaiah 6, Psalm 29, John 3)
Sovereign of the universe,
    touch us with your splendid presence.
Reveal yourself to us, O mystery that beckons.
Draw us into your hopeful plans,
    for us and for all,
        through Jesus Christ our Riddle Maker and Savior,
        and through the Spirit Wind, Midwife unto new life.
Amen.

THANKSGIVING AND COMMUNION

Invitation to the Offering (Romans 8)
Through the miracle of new life given to each of us, we have been adopted into the family of God. More than this, we are heirs to the blessings of God's power, wisdom, and love. So let us share our bounty with others, that we may welcome more into our family. Let us give to our brothers and sisters, in the name of Jesus Christ, our eldest brother.

Offering Prayer (John 3, Romans 8)
> It is only because of Jesus Christ
>> that we are bold enough
>>> to call you Father and Mother,
>>>> O Sovereign of the Universe.
> We do so now,
>> to remind ourselves of our many sisters and brothers,
>> your many children, who need hope and care.
> Use our gifts to reach others
>> with the story of your great love
>>> for our world. Amen.

SENDING FORTH

Benediction (Isaiah 6, Psalm 29, John 3, Romans 8)
(Have three people deliver benediction from three different locations amidst the congregation or sanctuary.)

Voice 1:   Look for the signs of the holy and mysterious one everywhere!

Voice 2:   Listen for the sound of seraph wings and voices.

Voice 3:   Feel the trembling beneath your feet that heralds heavenly voices.

Voice 1:   Know that these mysteries have already entered your very lives and beings, children of God! More mysteries await you.

Voice 2:   May the Holy and Mysterious One visit you this week.

Voice 3:   And may the Holy and Mysterious One give you every strength and peace.

All: **Amen.**

CONTEMPORARY OPTIONS

Contemporary Gathering Words (Isaiah 6, Psalm 29)
We stand in the presence of God, Sovereign of the Universe, Lord of Hosts!
> **The whole earth is full of God's glory!**

God's voice peals like thunder over the waters,
the deserts, the forests!
The whole earth is full of God's glory!
Do you hear the angels' loud praise and feel
the shaking of the very foundations of this place?
God's presence surrounds us, fills this very place!
Holy, holy, holy is the Lord of hosts!

Praise Sentences (Isaiah 6, John 3, Romans 8)

The Sovereign of Hosts calls out, "Whom shall I send?
Who will go for us?"
Here am I. Send me!
Jesus Christ, heir of God, seeks his sisters and brothers.
We are the children of God, our Father and Mother.
The wind blows where it chooses!
O Spirit Wind, choose me!

JUNE 14, 2009

Second Sunday after Pentecost

B. J. Beu

COLOR
Green

SCRIPTURE READINGS
1 Samuel 15:34–16:13; Psalm 20; 2 Corinthians 5:6-10 (11-13) 14-17; Mark 4:26-34

THEME IDEAS
It is only with the heart that one can see rightly. This truth is witnessed in God's decision to anoint David as the new king of Israel: "The LORD does not see as mortals see; they look on the outward appearance, but the LORD looks on the heart" (1 Samuel 16:7b). This truth is proclaimed by Paul in his insistence, "We walk by faith, not by sight" (2 Corinthians 5:7). And it is expressed by Jesus, as he compares the kingdom of God to a tiny mustard seed where birds will one day make their nests. These scriptures teach us to see with the heart, that God may grant us our hearts' true desire.

INVITATION AND GATHERING

Call to Worship (Psalm 20, 2 Corinthians 5)
Come to the Lord.
We will walk in the light of faith.

Come to the Lord.
We will love in the light of faith.
Come to the Lord.
We will sing in the light of faith.
Come to the Lord.
We will live in the light of faith.

Opening Prayer (1 Samuel 15–16, Mark 4)

Be thou our vision, O God.
Help us walk by faith,
    not by sight.
Like Samuel before us,
    remind us once more
        that you do not see as mortals see,
        for you do not judge by outward appearances,
            but look on the heart.
Create a clean heart within us, O God,
    that we may see your kingdom
        in a tiny mustard seed
        and marvel at the simple beauty
            of our world and our lives. Amen.

PROCLAMATION AND RESPONSE

Prayer of Confession (1 Samuel 15–16, 2 Corinthians 5)

Living God,
    we have a hard time letting go—
        we cling to past dreams,
        we grieve over past losses,
        we weep for what might have been.
Like Samuel, who grieved over Saul
    when you rejected him in favor of David,
    we too cling to our grief
        and fail to see the new possibilities
            you put before us.
Help us walk by faith, not by sight,
    that we may see with your eyes,
        and be guided by our hearts. Amen.

Words of Assurance (2 Corinthians 5:17)
Hear the words of the Apostle Paul:
> "So if anyone is in Christ, there is a new creation:
> everything old has passed away;
> see, everything has become new!"

Invitation to the Word (1 Samuel 15–16, 2 Corinthians 5)
May the One who calls us to walk by faith, not by sight, open our hearts to hear the word of God. May the One who judges the heart, not outward appearances, guide our ears to hear what is truly the word of the Lord.

Call to Prayer (Psalm 20)
God hears our petitions and answers the pleas of the righteous. The ungodly place their confidence in the powers of this world, but our confidence is in the name of the Lord, our God. The powers of this world collapse and fall, but those who hope in the Lord shall rise and stand upright. Hear our prayers, O God, and hearken to our need.

THANKSGIVING AND COMMUNION

Offering Prayer (Mark 4)
Bountiful God,
> your kingdom is like seed
> > that someone scatters on the ground.
How it grows, we know not,
> but there is abundance in the harvest.
Your kingdom is like a tiny mustard seed
> that grows into a shrub
> where the birds of the air
> > build their nests.
May the gifts we bring
> bear as much fruit
> > as the seeds of your kingdom,
> > > that all may be fed
> > > and all may be blessed. Amen.

SENDING FORTH

Benediction (2 Corinthians 5)
The old has passed away,
and everything has become new.
In Christ, we are a new creation.
Walk, in the light of faith.
Our hearts light the way.
Love, in the light of faith.
Our hearts light the way.
Go forth, in the light of faith.
Our hearts light the way.

CONTEMPORARY OPTIONS

Contemporary Gathering Words (2 Corinthians 5)
Do you know where to go?
We travel familiar ground.
Do you see the path clearly?
We could walk it blindfold.
What does your heart tell you?
Walk by faith, not by sight.
It is only with the heart that one can see rightly.
We worship Christ, who is our path.

Praise Sentences (2 Corinthians 5; Psalm 147)
Our hope is in the name of the Lord, our God!
In Christ, we are a new creation.
Our hope is in the name of the Lord, our God!
We walk by faith, not by sight.
Our hope is in the name of the Lord, our God!
In Christ, we are a new creation.
Our hope is in the name of the Lord, our God!

JUNE 21, 2009

Third Sunday after Pentecost/Father's Day

Hans Holznagel

COLOR
Green

SCRIPTURE READINGS
1 Samuel 17:(1a, 4-11, 19-23) 32-49; Psalm 9:9-20; 2 Corinthians 6:1-13; Mark 4:35-41

THEME IDEAS
Battles, vengeance, adversity, and suffering are plentiful in today's readings. Those seeking an alternative theme might consider this subtheme: the power of the unexpected and the surprising. An elder, Saul, takes a chance on a confident young David, who wisely sheds conventional armor. In Psalm 9, God takes the side of the oppressed, needy, and poor, and is asked to declare nations "only human." In rebuking a storm, Jesus speaks the word "peace." In a dispute with the Corinthians, Paul issues an appeal to and from the heart.

INVITATION AND GATHERING

Call to Worship (Psalm 9)
Seek God; know God; trust God, O people.
Sing praises to the Lord, who dwells in Zion.

Declare God's deeds among the people,
for the needy are remembered, the poor have hope.
Sing praises to the Lord, who dwells in Zion.

Opening Prayer (1 Samuel 17, Psalm 9, 2 Corinthians 6, Mark 4)

Center us, O God,
to worship you this day.
Remove our needless armor.
Be our stronghold.
Grant us calm.
Give us joyful hearts and ready minds,
that we may be open to your grace. Amen.

PROCLAMATION AND RESPONSE

Prayer of Confession (Mark 4)

Merciful God,
when lashed by life's windstorms
we often lash out in return.
Forgive us
when we blame you or others
for our troubles.
Teach us to find you
in the eye of the storm.
Show us the calm center
that comes from a word of peace.

Words of Assurance (2 Corinthians 6)

Hear the witness of scripture:
God listens; God helps. Now is the day of salvation.
Open wide your hearts and receive God's forgiveness.
Amen.

Passing the Peace of Christ (Mark 4)

A word of peace can have awesome power. Let us share
signs of this peace in the name of the One we follow.
The peace of Christ be with you.
And also with you.

Invitation to the Word (Mark 4, 2 Corinthians 6)

Gracious God, great Teacher, Bearer of peace,
  we seek your wisdom.
Open our hearts and minds to your word
  and to possibilities yet unseen. Amen.

THANKSGIVING AND COMMUNION

Invitation to the Offering (Psalm 9, 2 Corinthians 6)

With the Apostle Paul, let us not "accept the grace of God
in vain." With the psalmist, let us praise and rejoice in
God, our stronghold in times of trouble and need. In gratitude for what we have received, let us bring our tithes
and our offerings.

Offering Prayer (1 Samuel 17)

Merciful God,
    we thank you for the many ways
      that gifts are offered in your service;
    we especially thank you for fathers and elders
      whose love and wisdom
        have touched our lives and our church.
Help the elders among us
    nurture the young in our midst,
      just as Saul took a chance on young David.
Help the young among us
    honor their elders,
      even as they are true to their own callings.
Accept our gifts, we pray,
    and bless now this morning's offerings,
    that we might do your will
      in this place and in all the world. Amen.

SENDING FORTH

Benediction (2 Corinthians 6)

Put obstacles in no one's way,
    but rejoice in purity, knowledge, patience, kindness,
    holiness of spirit, genuine love, truthful speech,

and the power of God.
Go in peace.

CONTEMPORARY OPTIONS

Contemporary Gathering Words (1 Samuel 17, Psalm 9, 2 Corinthians 6, Mark 4)

You're not what we expect, O Lord.
Victory without a sword,
   windstorms calmed with simple words,
   sleepless nights rewarded.
Help us put our trust in you,
   unexpected God.

Praise Sentences (Psalm 9)

Sing praise to God, who heeds our tears.
Sing praise to God, who helps the afflicted.
Sing praise to God, who lifts up the oppressed.
Sing praise to God, who remembers the needy.
Sing praise to God, who gives aid to the poor.
Sing praise to God, who is worthy of our thanks!

JUNE 28, 2009

Fourth Sunday after Pentecost
Mary Petrina Boyd

COLOR
Green

SCRIPTURE READINGS
2 Samuel 1:1, 17-27; Psalm 130; 2 Corinthians 8:7-15; Mark 5:21-43

THEME IDEAS
Today's texts address the reality of human suffering: lives lost in battle, the debilitating cost of chronic disease, the death of a child, the cry of despair. God comes to those in pain with healing and grace, restoring life and hope, offering the abundance of steadfast love, bringing peace to troubled souls. This is the vision of living in *shalom*, a world of God's peace, where all find healing and peace and where everyone has enough to thrive. In response to God's amazing gifts, we are called to build that community as we live generous lives, offering from our abundance, that others might simply live.

INVITATION AND GATHERING

Call to Worship (Psalm 130)
Wait for the Lord, like those who hope in God's mercy.
God's steadfast love endures forever.

Watch for God, like those who eagerly await the morning.
We watch for God, whose power redeems us.
Hear God's hopeful word, like those who long for pardon.
Sing praise to God and rejoice in God's love.

Opening Prayer (Mark 5)

Loving God,
we are yours.
We come as we are,
with our cares and concerns.
We long to touch you
and find healing in your embrace.
Strengthen our faith
and heal our brokenness,
that we may worship you with joy. Amen.

PROCLAMATION AND RESPONSE

Prayer of Confession (Psalm 130, Mark 5)

Out of the depths of despair,
we cry to you, O God.
We are lost in a world
of pain and suffering.
When we put our trust in weapons of war,
we find no peace.
When we put our faith in our own resources,
we feel the ache of our true needs.
When we put our hope in the health of our bodies,
we suffer pain and find no healing.
Come to us, O God.
Forgive our doubts and fears.
Heal our brokenness,
that we may rejoice in your steadfast love. Amen.

Words of Assurance (Psalm 130)

There is forgiveness and healing with God.
God's steadfast love
has the power to redeem our brokenness
and make us whole.

Passing the Peace of Christ (Mark 5)

The love of Christ touches every person, transforming us with grace. Greet your sisters and brothers with this love. Share God's peace.

Response to the Word (2 Samuel, 2 Corinthians 8, Mark 5)

Loving God,
let your word speak to our hearts.
Come and heal our brokenness
and restore us to life.
Comfort our grieving hearts.
Teach us to share from our abundance.
By your word,
transform us into your holy people. Amen.

THANKSGIVING AND COMMUNION

Invitation to the Offering (2 Corinthians 8)

Paul challenged the church at Corinth to recognize their abundance, that they might share with those in need. God calls us to give out of our bounty, that all might have enough to live on without fear. With eager hearts, let us joyfully give out of our abundance.

Offering Prayer (2 Corinthians 8)

Gracious God,
we thank you for our present abundance
and for the many blessings
you have bestowed upon this community.
We thank you for our faith,
for our knowledge of you,
and for the assurance of your love.
May all these gifts be a blessing
to those in need. Amen.

SENDING FORTH

Benediction (Mark 5)
    Christ's touch has healed you.
    God's love has restored you.
    The Spirit goes with you.
    Go in peace to share the joy of God's love.

CONTEMPORARY OPTIONS

Contemporary Gathering Words (Mark 5)
    Come, bring your pain.
    Draw close to Christ.
    Reach out to touch Jesus.
    Find healing and peace in his love.

Praise Sentences (Psalm 130, Mark 5)
    God's love is steadfast.
    God's power is great!
    God heals our brokenness and gives us peace.

JULY 5, 2009

Fifth Sunday after Pentecost
Mary J. Scifres

COLOR

Green

SCRIPTURE READINGS

2 Samuel 5:1-5, 9-10; Psalm 48; 2 Corinthians 12:2-10; Mark 6:1-13

THEME IDEAS

Sent forth by God and Christ's disciples, we are called to proclaim repentance, teach God's love, and offer Christ's healing ministry. These scriptures warn us, however, that our gifts will not always be accepted; our ministries will not always be received. When faced with rejection, Christ was amazed at people's unbelief. Even so, Jesus traveled on and offered kindness and mercy to new friends and different communities. Even as we face hardships and rejection in the ministries we offer, we are called to shake the dust off of our feet and travel on, offering kindness and mercy, ministry and love, to new friends and different communities.

INVITATION AND GATHERING

Call to Worship (Mark 6)
Take off your shoes!
   We are standing on holy ground.

Shake off the dust!
We are ready to start afresh.
Let us worship God and receive Christ's teachings,
that we may be renewed and strengthened
to share God's love with the world.

Opening Prayer (Mark 6)

Holy God,
    come into our village
      and teach us to be your people.
As we receive your word
    and rejoice in your grace,
    grant us the courage
      to share the message of your love.
Guide us out of the darkness
    of doubt and confusion
    and into the light of faith and hope,
      that we may share your light with the world.
In Christ's name, we pray. Amen.

PROCLAMATION AND RESPONSE

Prayer of Confession (Mark 6)

Merciful God,
    forgive us when we are paralyzed
      by confusion and doubt.
Strengthen our faith,
    that we may not only believe,
    but may be filled with the power
      to help and heal.
When others reject or refuse our ministry,
    help us to be forgiving and grace-filled.
Grant us the courage
    to accept those things that cannot be changed,
      that we may be freed from anger and resentment.
Forgive us when our disappointment
    clouds our wisdom
      and confuses our actions.

Guide us on this path of ministry,
   that we may be filled
      with the joy of our ministry. Amen.

Words of Assurance (2 Corinthians 12)

God's grace is sufficient for all our needs,
   covering all our sins.
God's power is made perfect in our weakness,
   as Christ redeems our lives
      and reconciles us fully and completely to God.
Amen and amen.

Passing the Peace of Christ (Mark 6)

Sent out in pairs, the first disciples were given authority
and power to do great deeds. Let us turn to our fellow disciples, offering words of love and grace, that we too may
be sent in pairs with power and authority, to do great
deeds with great love.

Response to the Word or Benediction (Mark 6)

Send us forth, O God,
   to do your work in the world.
Empower us to be your disciples.
Guide the paths of our lives,
   that we may enter into the towns and villages
      where our ministries are most needed
         and most readily received.
Encourage us to shake off the dust
   when our time is done or our ministries are rejected,
      that we may move forward into new opportunities
         for loving and healing others.

THANKSGIVING AND COMMUNION

The Great Thanksgiving (2 Samuel 5, 2 Corinthians 12, Mark 6)

It is right and a good and joyful thing,
   always and everywhere, to give thanks to you,
   Mighty God, our Comforter and Sustainer.

You made us in your image, to love and be loved.
When our love failed, your love remained steadfast.
You delivered us from captivity in Egypt,
    made covenant, time and again, to be our God,
    that we might be your people.
In the lineage of Abraham and Sarah,
    David and Bathsheba, Paul and Peter,
    we come now with gratitude and praise
    for your mighty acts of salvation
    and your generous covenant of love.
And so, with your people on earth
    and all the company of heaven,
    we praise your name and join their unending hymn:
    Holy, holy, holy Lord, God of power and might,
        heaven and earth are full of your glory.
    Hosanna in the highest!
    Blessed is the one who comes
        in the name of the Lord.
    Hosanna in the highest!
Holy are you, and blessed is your Son, Jesus Christ.
Your Spirit anointed him to preach good news to the poor,
    to offer healing and mercy to the sick,
    to proclaim repentance and forgiveness of sins,
    and to share your love with the world.
Through Christ and the Holy Spirit,
    you gave birth to the church,
    delivered us from slavery to sin and death,
    and made with us a new covenant
    by water and the Spirit.
Christ commissioned us to be disciples of healing
    and hope to a world in need.
As we sit at this table, you nurture us to live
    this commission with your bread of life
    and living water.
On the night when Jesus last ate with his disciples,
    he took bread, blessed it and broke it,
    and gave it to the disciples, saying,

"Take, eat; this is my body."
Then Jesus took the cup, gave thanks to you,
     gave it to the disciples, and said:
     "This is my blood of the new covenant,
     which is poured out for many.
     Truly I tell you, I will never again drink
     of the fruit of the vine until that day
     when I drink it new in the kingdom of God."
And so, in remembrance of these,
     your mighty acts in Christ Jesus,
     we offer ourselves in praise and thanksgiving
     as a holy and living gift to you and to your world.
In union with Christ's gift of love to us and to your world,
     we proclaim the mystery of faith.
     Christ has died. Christ is risen.
     Christ will come again.

Communion Prayer (Mark 6)

Pour out your Holy Spirit
     on all of us gathered here
         and on these gifts of bread and wine.
Make them be for us the life and love of Christ,
     that we may be disciples of Christ for the world,
         redeemed by your love and grace.
By your Spirit, make us one with Christ,
     one with each other,
         and one in ministry to all the world.
May we proclaim your love and your hope
     until Christ comes in final victory,
         when we will drink of the fruit of the vine
         and feast at your heavenly banquet.
Through Jesus the Christ,
     together with the Holy Spirit,
         all honor and glory is yours, almighty God,
             now and forever. Amen.

SENDING FORTH

Benediction (Mark 6)

Shake off the dust!
We go forth with the power of God.
Proclaim the word of the Lord.
We go out as Christ's disciples.

CONTEMPORARY OPTIONS

Contemporary Gathering Words (Psalm 48, Mark 6)

God's name reaches out to the ends of the earth.
Great is the name of the Lord!
God's mercy extends to the ends of the earth.
Great is the name of the Lord!
God's guidance embraces the ends of the earth.
Great is the name of the Lord!
God's love calls us here to be refreshed and renewed.
Great is the name of the Lord!

Praise Sentences (Psalm 48)

Great is the Lord and greatly to be praised.
Great is the Lord our God!
Great is the Lord and greatly to be praised.
Great is the Lord our God!

JULY 12, 2009

Sixth Sunday after Pentecost
Ciona D. Rouse

COLOR
Green

SCRIPTURE READINGS
2 Samuel 6:1-5, 12b-19; Psalm 24; Ephesians 1:3-14; Mark 6:14-29

THEME IDEAS
In the presence of God, King David could not help but release his inhibitions and praise God with all that he was. He danced without shame, even if people thought he was undignified. He danced before the Lord! Just as the ark of the covenant served as a symbol of God's presence for the Israelites, all of creation reminds us that God is with us. Our very breath exists because God created us, and all of creation belongs to God, as the psalmist proclaims. For this, we rejoice and praise God, like David danced and sang! Through the gift of the Holy Spirit, mentioned in Ephesians, we are reminded that God has not abandoned us. We are children of God through Jesus Christ. By sending the Holy Spirit, God guides us according to God's will. For this, we rejoice and praise! As the church, we are called to dance, shout, pray, live, and serve in praise of God's glory!

INVITATION AND GATHERING

Call to Worship (2 Samuel 6)
(Consider alternating between men and women, children and youth.)
We come here shouting, our voices lifted in praise.
We come here singing, our songs full of joy.
We come here dancing, our hearts rejoicing.
To the Holy One who is worthy,
all praise and glory forevermore!

Opening Prayer (2 Samuel 6)
Lord of the dance,
  creator of whirling winds
    and shimmering flames,
      move in us this day.
Breathe life into our songs of praise.
Set our hearts ablaze to your word.
May our worship
  bring joy to you, Lord.
In Christ's name we pray, Amen.

PROCLAMATION AND RESPONSE

Prayer of Confession (Ephesians 1, Psalm 24, 2 Samuel 6)
You have called us by name, Lord,
  and made us your family.
Yet we do not always live
  as one body in Christ—
    we neglect to care for your creation;
    we forget that our neighbor is also our sister;
    we ignore suffering children in lands far away.
Forgive us, we pray.
Loosen the chains
  we place on our lives—
    chains of burden and busyness,
    chains of ignorance and stress.
Free us to care for your family,

that we all might dance, sing,
   and praise your glorious name! Amen.

Words of Assurance (Psalm 24, Mark 6)

We belong to the king of glory who joyfully sets us free.
In Christ's healing hands, you find forgiveness.
   In Christ's healing touch, you find forgiveness.
   Glory be to God! Amen.

Passing the Peace of Christ (Ephesians 1)

We are adopted as God's children through Jesus Christ.
We sit next to a sister, even when we know her as friend.
We sit next to a brother, even when we think him a
stranger. Turn now to your family in Christ and share with
them signs of Christ's love and peace.

Invitation to the Word (2 Samuel 6)

Just as King David danced unashamed as the ark of the
covenant was brought into Jerusalem, let our hearts dance
with unrestrained joy as we prepare to hear God's word
spoken afresh today.
(B. J. Beu)

THANKSGIVING AND COMMUNION

Offering Prayer (Psalm 24, Ephesians 1)

Creator of all things,
   we give back to you
      in praise of your glory.
We do not wish to simply praise you
   with our song and our words and our hands;
   we wish to praise you
      by loving our brothers and sisters in Christ.
Take and use our gifts,
   that they may serve your kingdom. Amen.

SENDING FORTH

Benediction

Children of God,
   go forth dancing, singing, and praising.

Dance joy into sorrowful places!
Sing hope into places of despair!
Praise God this day and always!

CONTEMPORARY OPTIONS

Contemporary Gathering Words

Our feet move because of your great worth!
Yes, Lord, we dance for the rest of our days!
Our hearts rejoice in song because of your goodness!
Yes, Lord, we sing for the rest of our days!
Our voices cry out because of your glory!
Yes, Lord, we shout for the rest of our days!
We praise you always for the rest of our days!

Praise Sentences

With our lives we will praise you, King of glory!
Who is the King of glory? Jesus, our Lord!

JULY 19, 2009

Seventh Sunday after Pentecost

B. J. Beu

COLOR
Green

SCRIPTURE READINGS
2 Samuel 7:1-14a; Psalm 89:20-37; Ephesians 2:11-22; Mark 6:30-34, 53-56

THEME IDEAS
What do we do when God's promises are broken? What 2 Samuel states simply, Psalm 89 extols with great force: David's rule and lineage will never end. God will punish Israel's wrongdoing, but like the sun and the moon, David's line will endure forever. What happened? Perhaps God realized that the peace Israel hoped for in vanquishing its enemies was no real peace. The peace Jesus brought, the peace attested to in both Mark and Ephesians, is not accomplished by force of arms or family lineage, but by the love of a shepherd and by the reconciliation of enemies. Perhaps the biblical writers misunderstood God's promises to begin with. Perhaps true kingship and lineage come through shepherding love and by bringing enemies together in friendship and kinship, not by keeping them down and out.

INVITATION AND GATHERING

Call to Worship (Ephesians 2, Mark 6)

Come away, disciples of Christ, and rest from your labors.
We are weary from our work.
Come away, disciples of Christ, and leave the demands
of the crowds.
There are always more who need our help.
Come away, disciples of Christ, and be renewed
in fellowship with our shepherd.
We too love the sheep, but need our own renewal.
We too need to hear anew the teachings of Jesus,
to give us strength for the journey.
Come away, disciples of Christ, and draw courage
from the one who gives us peace.

Opening Prayer (Ephesians 2, Mark 6)

Reconciling God,
    proclaim peace to us once more.
Put to death all hostility within us
    and help us be one with our enemies,
    that we may all be members
        of your household.
Remove the animosities
    to which we cling
        and be our shepherd,
            even as we are the sheep of your pasture,
                through Jesus Christ,
                our guide and guardian. Amen.

PROCLAMATION AND RESPONSE

Prayer of Confession (2 Samuel 7, Psalm 89, Ephesians 2, Mark 6)

O God, the rock of our salvation,
    your faithfulness is as constant
        as the north star.
But your holiness frightens us—
    for the justice of your love

brings judgment on our lives.
Like David before us,
　　we would rather build you a temple
　　　and keep you safely in one place
　　　than have you move about with us in a tabernacle
　　　and be everywhere we go.
Like the psalmist,
　　we would rather shout the certainty of your favor—
　　　a favor as predictable as the rising sun and moon,
　　　than face the possibility that our peace may come,
　　　　not through strength of arms,
　　　　but through the love of a shepherd
　　　　　for the lost sheep of our world.

Words of Assurance (Ephesians 2)

In Christ, we are citizens with the saints
　　as members of the household of God.
In Christ, we are built spiritually
　　into a holy temple of the Lord,
　　a dwelling place for God.

Invitation to the Word (2 Samuel 7)

The Holy One of Israel, the one who dwelt in a tent, the one who traveled in an ark containing stone tablets etched with the Ten Commandments, is here with us today. Let us open our hearts and minds to hear again the words of faith spoken by God's people since the days of the kings of old.

Call to Prayer (Mark 6)

As Jesus had compassion for the people of his day, for they were like sheep without a shepherd, so Jesus has compassion for us today. We too are in need of a shepherd to guide us and to give us rest. Come; let us share our burdens and our joys with the Lord. Let us share our prayers with the One who brings us peace.

THANKSGIVING AND COMMUNION

Offering Prayer (2 Samuel 7, Ephesians 2, Mark 6)
God of steadfast love,
>   when Israel was not a people,
>>   you made them into a great nation;
>   when David rested from the labor
>>   of protecting and defending your people,
>>>   you built him a house of cedar.
You bless your people in ways beyond count
>   and lead us to become shepherds for others,
>>   even as Jesus is our shepherd.
Bless our tithes and offerings,
>   that they may be signs of our worthiness
>>   as to be members of your household
>>>   with the great saints that have gone before us.

SENDING FORTH

Benediction (Ephesians 2)
The old differences have died away.
>   **Christ has made us one.**
The old arguments have lost their appeal.
>   **Christ has brought us peace.**
The old hatreds have been swallowed up.
>   **Christ has brought us love.**

CONTEMPORARY OPTIONS

Contemporary Gathering Words (Mark 6)
We're lost and can't find our way home.
Who will be our shepherd?
>   **Jesus is our shepherd.**
We're hurt and don't know where to turn.
Who will tend our wounds?
>   **Jesus is our shepherd.**
We're anxious and stressed out.
Who will ease our troubled minds?

Jesus is our shepherd.
Praise God for Jesus!
Praise God for our shepherd!

Praise Sentences (Psalm 89, Mark 6)

Jesus is our shepherd.
Jesus brings us peace.
God is greatly to be exalted!
God's steadfast love endures forever!
Jesus is our shepherd.
Jesus brings us peace.

JULY 26, 2009

Eighth Sunday after Pentecost

B. J. Beu

COLOR

Green

SCRIPTURE READINGS

2 Samuel 11:1-15; Psalm 14; Ephesians 3:14-21; John 6:1-21

THEME IDEAS

How do we bring people to God? Scripture records God's abiding love for King David—the king who loved God dearly and who was faithful. Yet we find David sending out his soldiers to fight and die for king and country, and while they die, he commits adultery with Bathsheba. Then, when she becomes pregnant, this pious man of God makes sure her husband is killed in battle. When God's faithful act in such a way, is there any wonder "fools say in their hearts, 'There is no God'" (Psalm 14:1)? Is there any wonder people say, "I'd be a Christian if it weren't for the Christians"? We can celebrate with Paul that all the families of the earth take their name in God; and that, through Christ, we discover God's love. But until we have an experience of Jesus, until we have an encounter with the One who feeds us and gathers up the fragments of our lives, that nothing may be lost, we will be turned off by well-speaking, and well-spoken-of, hypocrites of the faith.

INVITATION AND GATHERING

Call to Worship (John 6)

Why have you come to this place?
We have come to find Jesus.
Why have you come today?
We are tired in body and spirit.
Jesus bids you sit and be at ease.
We are hungry with nothing to eat.
Come and eat your fill.
But there are only five barley loaves and two fish.
There is plenty for all.
Will we find wholeness here?
Jesus gathers the fragments of our lives,
that nothing may be lost.

Opening Prayer (John 6)

God of our hopes and dreams,
  we are empty, and long to be filled;
  we are hungry, and long to be fed;
  we are lost, and long to be found.
Gather us into your love,
  and pick up the pieces of our lives,
  just as Jesus gathered up the fragments
    of the five loaves and two fish
    that remained after feeding the five thousand.
Call us anew to eat our fill
  and to find our true nourishment in Jesus,
    the bread of heaven. Amen.

PROCLAMATION AND RESPONSE

Prayer of Confession (2 Samuel 11, Psalm 14)

God of steadfast love,
  fools say in their hearts:
    "There is no God."
How often, O Lord,
  are we the fools

who confess you with our lips,
but deny you with our actions?
How often do we act as if you sleep, O God,
confident that you know not what we do?
How often, like King David before us,
do we seek to hide the fruit of our sin,
just as David had Bathsheba's husband killed
rather than confess his transgression?
How often do we cause others to stumble,
when we act hypocritically in our faith?
Help us be constant as the north star, O God,
that others have no occasion
to witness our example and say:
"I'd be a Christian
if it weren't for the Christians."

Words of Assurance (Psalm 14)

When God restored the fortunes of Zion,
they were like people who dream—
people who rejoiced and were glad.
As God restores our fortunes,
let us join them in their glad song
and in their rejoicing.

Invitation to the Word (Ephesians 3:18-19)

With the church at Ephesus, may we hear anew the words
of Paul: "I pray that you may have the power to comprehend, with all the saints, what is the breadth and length
and height and depth, and to know the love of Christ that
surpasses knowledge, so that you may be filled with all
the fullness of God."

Call to Prayer (Ephesians 3)

Let us lift up our prayers through Jesus Christ our Lord,
who, by the power of the Holy Spirit at work within us, is
able to accomplish far more than all we can ask or imagine. All glory and honor to the one who hears and answers
our prayers.

THANKSGIVING AND COMMUNION

Offering Prayer (John 6)
God of abundant love,
     in you, nothing is lost.
Gather our offerings,
     as Jesus gathered up the baskets
         of leftover food.
Gather our efforts,
     as Jesus gathered the hopes
         of the people who looked for a true king.
Gather our service,
     as Jesus gathered people
         to God's heavenly banquet.
Bless the offerings we have gathered,
     that nothing may be lost. Amen.

SENDING FORTH

Benediction (Psalm 14, John 6)
Fools say in their hearts: "There is no God."
     We have found Jesus, who gives us the bread of life.
Fools say in their hearts: "All believers are hypocrites."
     **We have found Jesus, who strengthens us in our
     inner being, through the power of God's Spirit.**
Fools say in their hearts: "There is no hope in heaven."
     **We have found Jesus, who gathers the fragments
     of our lives, that nothing may be lost.**

CONTEMPORARY OPTIONS

Contemporary Gathering Words (Psalm 14, John 6)
Rejoice, folks, Jesus is in our midst.
     Feed us, Jesus, and fill us with hope.
Be glad, friends, Jesus has bread and fish to spare.
     **Free us, Jesus, from the pursuit of food
     that does not satisfy.**
Sing for joy, people of God; God gathers up the pieces

of our lives, that nothing may be lost.
Thanks be to God!

Praise Sentences (Ephesians 3, John 6)
Jesus feeds the multitudes.
We are rooted in God's love.
Jesus brings us hope.
We are strengthened by God's Spirit.
Jesus gathers the lost and the scattered.
We are rooted in God's love.
In Jesus, we are made whole.

AUGUST 2, 2009

Ninth Sunday after Pentecost

Mary J. Scifres

COLOR

Green

SCRIPTURE READINGS

2 Samuel 11:26–12:13a; Psalm 51:1-12; Ephesians 4:1-16;
John 6:24-35

THEME IDEAS

Leading a life worthy of God's blessings and calling is not
an easy task. Even King David, blessed with riches and
wives, failed as he stole another man's wife and then had
the man murdered. Yet, God calls to us still, offering the
grace to use our gifts for building the body of Christ, for
strengthening and building God's great love—the church.
As we reflect upon the gifts we are given, we are reminded that God's grace comes to us as the bread of life,
as the water that quenches every thirst, as the nourishment of Christ Jesus in our lives—always giving, always
strengthening, always feeding our greatest needs. When
we receive this blessing of gracious nourishment from
Christ, we are then able to truly lead lives worthy of the
calling to which we have been called.

INVITATION AND GATHERING

Call to Worship (Ephesians 4)

With patience and love, we come as one family.
We are one body of Christ, united in God.
Come! Speak of truth, truth told in love.
We gather to listen, and to share our stories.
We are God's children, parts of Christ's purpose.
**We rejoice in our gifts, and we thank God
for this grace.**
Come! Now is the time to worship.

Opening Prayer (Ephesians 4)

God of unity and peace,
> bind us together
> > as we come now to worship.
Strengthen the ties
> that make us your family.
Grant us the grace to recognize our gifts
> and our place in this body.
Guide us to hear your calling
> as you speak to our lives.
Encourage us to bravely burst forth
> as pastors and teachers, prophets and healers,
> > evangelists and leaders.
Dwell in our very hearts,
> that we may serve in humility—
> > braided with strength and gentleness,
> > intertwined with passion.
Build us up in love,
> that we may grow in our knowledge
> and our love of you.
Speak your truth to our lives,
> that we may lead lives
> > worthy of your calling. Amen.

Affirmation of Faith (Ephesians 4)

There is one hope, one calling, to which we are called.
The hope in our lives is Jesus.

There is one hope, one calling, to which we are called.
The call we must answer is God's.
There is one faith, one hope, one Lord of us all.
The Lord of our lives is Jesus.
There is one baptism, one Father, one Mother of all.
The creator who calls us is God.
We are one body, one family, one church,
woven by the Spirit with bonds of peace.
With Christ's children throughout all of this earth,
we are one body in unity and love.

PROCLAMATION AND RESPONSE

Prayer of Confession (Psalm 51)
Have mercy on us,
  O God of love and grace.
Wash away the thoughts
  that bind us to sin
  and erase those actions
    that lead us away from you.
Teach us your wisdom
  and put a new spirit
    of truth and love and righteousness
      within us.
Fill us with the joy you offer
  through the grace of Jesus Christ.
Grant us clean hearts and willing minds,
  that we may walk in your ways
    and rejoice in your truth.
Strengthen us
  with loving plans and righteous deeds,
  that we may offer your justice and mercy
    to a world in need. Amen.

—Or—

Prayer of Confession (Ephesians 4)
God of unity and love,
  place within each of us

a spirit of hope and community.
Have mercy upon us
    when we speak without love
        or act without humility.
Cleanse us with the living water of your grace.
Create in us willing hearts
    to live in patience and gentleness.
Raise us up to be your children,
    growing toward maturity
        in faith and love.
Strengthen this church,
    that we may be a model
        of ministry and unity
            for all the world to see.
In Christ's name, we pray. Amen.

Words of Assurance (Ephesians 4, John 6)

Know, dear friends, that we are knit together
    by the very bonds of Christ's love for us.
As the living water, Christ washes us clean
    and makes us a new creation.
As our bread of life, Christ nurtures and sustains us.
Because we believe, we need never hunger
    or thirst for mercy.
Forgiveness is ours, both now and forevermore. Amen.

Passing the Peace of Christ (Ephesians 4)

Lead lives worthy of the calling to which you have been called. Share together signs of humility and gentleness—signs of love and grace. Be for one another the very presence of God in this room. Be the very peace of Christ as we greet our neighbors.

Response to the Word (Ephesians 4)

Lead lives worthy of God's call.
    We will embrace one another in love and grace.
Act with patience, humility, and gentleness.
    We will live together in unity and peace.
Speak the truth in love, building a church of love.

In Christ, we will follow God's lead in all that we do.
Strengthen this body of Christ, working together as one.
**We will build a world of love, joined together
with Christ.**

THANKSGIVING AND COMMUNION

Invitation to the Offering (Ephesians 4)
Pastor or prophet, teacher or nurse, poor man or rich
woman, each of us is called to build up the body of Christ.
Our job is unfinished until each of us has come to maturity in the full stature of Christ Jesus. Bring now your gifts,
given to us by the grace of God.

Offering Prayer (Ephesians 4, John 6)
God of miraculous grace,
    transform our gifts
        into the work of ministry.
Transform our lives
    into your presence in the world.
Through these gifts,
    may we grow in the knowledge of Christ
        and be strengthened in the unity of faith.
Transform these gifts into the bread of life
    so that in our giving
        others may be fed.
Make these gifts the waters
    that spring up into eternal life,
    so that in our giving,
        others may be nurtured and strengthened
            as children of God.
In your loving and nurturing name,
    we pray. Amen.

SENDING FORTH

Benediction (Ephesians 4)
Go forth to lead lives worthy of Christ's call.
Joined together as one, we are strengthened

to share our gifts with the world.
Make every effort to maintain this unity.
Knit together by Christ, we are ready to serve!

CONTEMPORARY OPTIONS

Contemporary Gathering Words (Ephesians 4)
The Spirit weaves us together.
Even the broken threads of our lives
can be trimmed and melded.
Even the tattered seams
can be mended and joined.
Diverse colors, various patterns,
and unique fabrics ...
all are welcome here!
Bring now your gifts,
amazing and broken.
Bring now yourselves,
awesome and torn.
Humility and gentleness,
patience and perseverance ...
all are a part of this place.
Make now an effort to find this new unity.
Take now a step into this body,
bound by God's peace.
May the Spirit weave us together
with one hope and one faith,
bound together in unity and love.

Praise Sentences (Ephesians 4)
There is one Lord, one faith, one baptism,
one hope of our calling, one God of us all!
There is one Spirit, one body, one Savior in Christ,
one hope of our calling, one God of us all!

AUGUST 9, 2009

Tenth Sunday after Pentecost
John A. Brewer

COLOR
Green

SCRIPTURE READINGS
2 Samuel 18:5-9, 15, 31-33; Psalm 130; Ephesians 4:25–5:2; John 6:35, 41-51

THEME IDEAS
These texts lend themselves to a number of mid-summer themes, including the grief of war, the forgiveness of God, patience in listening for the direction of God, spiritual hunger that is fed only by bread from heaven, and the encouragement to live a life of integrity and authenticity as followers of Christ. Vietnam, Afghanistan, and Iraq are all indications of an impatient world that is hungering for something beyond our reach. So, God reaches out to us in our humanness and gives us this example, this person, this Christ.

INVITATION AND GATHERING

Call to Worship (Psalm 130)
Out of the depths I cry to you.
Lord, hear my voice.
Let your ears be attentive to my cry for mercy.

If you kept a record of sins, Lord,
who could stand?
But with you there is forgiveness,
that we might serve you with reverence.
I wait for the Lord, my whole being waits,
and in God's word I put my hope.
Israel, put your hope in the Lord
and in God's unfailing love.
Out of the depths I cry to you.
Lord, hear my voice.

Opening Prayer (John 6, Psalm 130)
O Bread of heaven,
come down.
Come down and fill us with your Spirit—
for your Spirit satisfies like no other.
We hunger and thirst for you this morning
and long to be nurtured
in your love and forgiveness.
So we come to this sacred time and place,
where our hungers are finally and fully satisfied
as only your bread can do.
We will wait and listen
for your leading in this hour. Amen.

PROCLAMATION AND RESPONSE

Prayer of Confession (2 Samuel, Psalm 130, Ephesians 4)
O God of compassion,
if you kept a record of our sins,
who could stand?
We come before you with our brokenness
and our wounds for all to see.
We bring our anger, our bitterness,
our unwholesome talk,
and our deceitfulness.
We try to do good,
but sometimes fail.

We choose to do evil,
and sometimes succeed.
Keep your promise to forgive us
when we confess to you completely.
Without you, we have no hope.

Words of Assurance (Psalm 130, John 6)

If we confess our sins, God is faithful and will forgive us.
God provides freely, in the bread of heaven,
all the mercy we need for life everlasting.
The good news is forgiveness in the name of Christ Jesus.

Passing the Peace of Christ (Ephesians 4)

We are not far from the kingdom of God. In fact, the kingdom of God is within you. Extend to those near you evidence of the kingdom in your greetings of peace and love.

Response to the Word (2 Samuel, John 6, Ephesians 4)

Glorious things of thee are spoken.
We marvel at the wisdom of your word,
O God of heaven.
May these words we have heard
become nourishment for our souls
and guidance for the living of our daily lives.
Write these words on our hearts, O Lord,
that we may be reflections of your truth and mercy.
Amen.

THANKSGIVING AND COMMUNION

Invitation to the Offering (Psalm 130, John 6)

Freely we have received. Thus, we freely give: grace upon grace. Let us express our love and appreciation to God, by extending the grace and mercy of God to a hungry world.

Offering Prayer (John 6, Ephesians 4)

O Lord, our Lord,
how majestic is your name in all the earth!
We bow before you and thank you for the privilege
to participate in your acts of kindness and love

here on earth.
May these gifts truly become instruments
of your purposes here in our church, our community,
and around the world. Amen.

SENDING FORTH

Benediction (2 Samuel, John 6, Ephesians 4)
Go forth and live as Christ in the world.
Speak and live with integrity
as you journey through this new week,
knowing that God will satisfy your every need
and lead you to a victorious life.

CONTEMPORARY OPTIONS

Contemporary Gathering Words (2 Samuel, Psalm 130)
You have been waiting long enough.
It's time to listen for God's voice.
We have been waiting many a long night.
Well, the day is here and the time is now
to find new hope in God alone!
**It is God! It is Jesus Christ, God himself,
who is finally saving us!**
Then come and join in the hope we share
of God's never-ending love.
We will celebrate by singing and praising God!

Praise Sentences
Totally, completely, without reservation,
God is worthy of our praise!
**Without holding anything back,
we sing and shout the praise of our God!**

AUGUST 16, 2009

Eleventh Sunday after Pentecost
Jamie D. Greening

COLOR
Green

SCRIPTURE READINGS
1 Kings 2:10-12; 3:3-14; Psalm 111; Ephesians 5:15-20; John 6:51-58

THEME IDEAS
The primary theme of these texts is the myriad ways God provides for our needs. The psalm highlights the provision of food and the covenant by recalling manna in the wilderness and the giving of the law at Sinai. The narrative of David's death indicates God's provision for an heir. In the Gospel of John, Christ provides his own flesh and blood as the gift of eternal life. Paul's letter to Ephesus reminds us that the provision of the Holy Spirit is from God. The secondary theme of these texts is our response to the provision of God through praise and thanksgiving.

INVITATION AND GATHERING

Call to Worship (Ephesians 5)
As we gather in this sacred moment for a sacred purpose, let us make the most of our time together.
We have come to worship the Lord our God.

As we sing psalms and hymns and spiritual songs,
let us make the most of our time together.
We have come to worship the Lord our God.
As we respond to the melody in our hearts,
let us make the most of our time together.
We have come to worship the Lord our God.

Opening Prayer (1 Kings 3)

O Lord our God,
though we are as little children,
not fully able to discern the spiritual forces
coming in and out of our lives,
you have chosen us as your people.
Give your servants understanding minds
to discern between the good and evil
surrounding us each day,
that we may choose what is good and pleasing
in your sight. Amen.

PROCLAMATION AND RESPONSE

Prayer of Confession (Ephesians 5, John 6, Psalm 111)

Lord, we have lived as unwise people.
God, forgive us for wasting time.
We have been foolish.
Jesus, forgive us for not understanding your will.
We have filled ourselves with the wine of worldliness.
Holy Spirit, forgive us for not being filled with you.
We have forsaken your spiritual food.
**Great Triune God of grace, forgive us for not drawing
our strength from your bread of heaven.**
Almighty God, please add to your mighty deeds
by forgiving our transgressions. Amen.

Words of Assurance (Psalm 111)

The Lord is gracious to us and gentle.
The Lord heals our souls with love.
The Lord is merciful,
providing spiritual food for the hungry.

Be healed in your hearts and be fed in your souls
  by the forgiveness found in Jesus Christ our Lord.

Passing the Peace of Christ (1 Kings 2, 3)

As the Lord provided peace for David's child Solomon,
God has provided peace for us as beloved sons and
daughters. Let us now bless one another with the peace
of God's presence.

Response to the Word (John 6)

We have heard the word of God today.
  It is a taste of the bread from heaven.
We have experienced the joy of worship.
  It is a taste of the cup of salvation.
We have experienced God's provision for our life.
  It is a taste of eternal life.

THANKSGIVING AND COMMUNION

Invitation to Communion (John 6)

In a world hungry from spiritual anemia, where can real
food be found? For those who starve for love, where can
unconditional and everlasting love be found? For those
who yearn for hope, where can hope be found? For those
who crave acceptance and tolerance, where can true acceptance and tolerance be found? Seek the food that God
has provided. Eat the bread of life, which has come down
from heaven. Drink the cup of salvation, the promise of
God's love. Eat, drink, and be satisfied.

Communion Liturgy (Ephesians 5)

Gathered around the communion meal,
we give thanks for food that truly satisfies.
  We give thanks through the singing
  of psalms, hymns, and spiritual songs.
Gathered around the Lord's table,
we give thanks for the gift of eternal life.
  We give thanks through the melody in our hearts
  and the joy in our souls.

Gathered around the heavenly banquet,
we give thanks for the tune of the ages,
even Jesus Christ our Lord.

SENDING FORTH

Benediction (1 Kings 3)

Grant us, O Lord, understanding minds,
that we might know how to live.
   Grant us discerning hearts,
   that we might know the difference
   between good and evil,
   and how we might live to please you.
Grant us, O Lord, peace and prosperity all our days,
to the glory of your name.

CONTEMPORARY OPTIONS

Contemporary Gathering Words (Ephesians 5)

Time slips away like water in the hand,
   or a balloon lifted into the sky.
We think there is plenty,
   but then it is gone, wasted.
So it is the will of God
   that we invest our time wisely
      in the divine work of worship.
Today we lift our voices and raise our hands,
   seeking to be filled with the Spirit,
      in the name of Jesus Christ.

Praise Sentences (Psalm 111)

Great are the works of the Lord,
They make our head spin with wonder!

Communion Poem, "Repose"

The altar table's meal is spread,
Holy Communion, wine and bread.
The minister preaches rising from the dead.
In solemn thought I bow my head.

The chalice catches bright sunshine,
filled with dark eucharistic wine.
Jesus Christ invites us to dine.
I feel the chill run down my spine.
On the floor in bended knee,
I give the Lord all of me.
With prayer made in sincerity,
My soul sobs for eternity.

AUGUST 23, 2009

Twelfth Sunday after Pentecost

B. J. Beu

COLOR

Green

SCRIPTURE READINGS

1 Kings 8:(1, 6, 10-11) 22-30, 41-43; Psalm 84; Ephesians 6:10-20; John 6:56-69

THEME IDEAS

With the exception of the reading from John, prayer is a unifying theme of these texts. Solomon prays at the dedication of the temple in Jerusalem; the psalmist prays for Israel and the joys of being in God's house; and Paul enjoins Christians to put on the full armor of God and pray in the Spirit at all times. To tie in the gospel reading, worship leaders could focus on how abiding in Christ is accomplished not only through the elements of Holy Communion, but also through prayer in the Spirit.

INVITATION AND GATHERING

Call to Worship (Psalm 84)
How lovely is your dwelling place, O Lord of hosts!
To you our hearts and souls sing for joy, O God.
Happy are those who live in your house, O Lord of hosts.
Happy are those whose strength is in you, O God.

It is better to be a doorkeeper in your house
than to live in the tents of wickedness.
O Lord of hosts, happy are those who trust in you.

Opening Prayer (1 Kings 8, Ephesians 6)
Holy One of mystery and power,
    there is no God like you
        in heaven above or on earth below,
        keeping covenant and steadfast love
          with all who walk before you
            with pure and upright hearts.
Fill our lives with your glory,
    as you filled the temple with cloud
        when Solomon first brought the ark
          into your holy dwelling place.
Give us the strength and the power
    to withstand the forces of evil
        at work in our lives and in our world. Amen.

PROCLAMATION AND RESPONSE

Prayer of Confession (1 Kings 8, Ephesians 6)
Mighty One of Israel,
    we walk in paths well trodden
        by generations of fellow believers.
We love to claim you as our God
    and to be known as your people.
We love to hear the great deeds of the saints
    who went before us.
We love to count ourselves
    in their mighty company.
Forgive our hesitancy
    to build our own monuments
        to your importance in our lives.
Forgive our reluctance
    to put on our own armor of faith
        as we face the powers of sin and death
          in our own lives. Amen.

Words of Assurance (Psalm 84)
The Lord God is a sun and shield,
> bestowing favor and honor and every good thing
> > on those who walk uprightly.
Trust in the Lord and receive God's blessings.

Invitation to the Word (John 6:68)
When Jesus' followers heard that to abide in him, they must partake of his body and blood, many turned and went away. The teaching was too difficult for them to bear. Yet, the words of Jesus are spirit and life. As we listen to God's word today, let us not look for easy answers, but affirm with Peter: "Lord, to whom can we go? You have the words of eternal life."

Call to Prayer (Psalm 84, Ephesians 6)
The Lord of hosts hears our prayers. The God of Jacob and Solomon and Paul and Peter gives ear to our petitions and our songs of thanksgiving. Let us lift up our prayers to the One who is our strength and our shield.

THANKSGIVING AND COMMUNION

Offering Prayer (Psalm 84)
Loving God,
> in your care
> > even the sparrow finds a home,
> > > and the swallow a nest for herself;
> in your care,
> > even the least of us finds life and spirit
> > and blessing upon blessing.
In gratitude for all we have received,
> accept our gifts and offerings,
> > that we may abide in your love. Amen.

SENDING FORTH

Benediction (Ephesians 6)
Be strong in the Lord and in the strength of God's power.
We will put on the full armor of God.

Withstand the spiritual arrows of darkness
and the temptations of this world.
We will fasten the belt of truth around our waist,
and put on the breastplate of righteousness.
Wear shoes to proclaim the gospel of peace.
Take the shield of faith and put on the helmet of salvation.
We will carry the sword of faith,
which is the word of God.
Be strong in the Lord and in the strength of God's power.

CONTEMPORARY OPTIONS

Contemporary Gathering Words (Psalm 84, John 6)
Life is hard. Evil is all around.
We are strong in the Lord.
The powers of darkness rise against us.
We stand firm in our God.
Put on the full armor of God.
We wear the belt of truth, the breastplate
of righteousness, the sword of faith,
and the helmet of salvation.
Life is hard. Evil is all around.
We are strong in the Lord.

Praise Sentences (Psalm 84)
Our hearts sing your praises, O God.
To you our souls sing for joy, O Lord.
Our spirits rejoice in your splendor.
Our hearts sing your praises, O God.
To you our souls sing for joy, O Lord.

AUGUST 30, 2009

Thirteenth Sunday after Pentecost
Mary Petrina Boyd

COLOR
Green

SCRIPTURE READINGS
Song of Solomon 2:8-13; Psalm 45:1-2, 6-9 (or Psalm 72); James 1:17-27; Mark 7:1-8, 14-15, 21-23

THEME IDEAS
Luscious imagery unites the passage from Song of Solomon with the psalm. We smell the fragrance of flowers and oil, hear birdsong and music, and see the beauty of God's world and the king's court. We are invited to come and be anointed with the oil of gladness. A world of such abundance calls us to live faithful lives filled with righteousness and equity—hating wickedness and all evil intentions, speaking carefully, and caring for those in need. God calls us to respond, not with outward ritual, but with a deep dedication of our hearts, embodying God's word in our actions.

INVITATION AND GATHERING

Call to Worship (Song of Solomon 2, Psalm 45)
Look to the mountains; look to the hills!
Love comes to us with joy!

The world is filled with beauty.
Flowers appear on the earth,
birdsong brightens the day.
Crops yield their produce in abundance,
the air is filled with sweetness.
The summer of God's love is with us.
Let the oil of gladness anoint your souls.
Arise and sing for joy!

Opening Prayer

Creating God,
you are the source of summer's splendor—
the beauty and fragrance of delicate flowers,
and sweet sound of birdsong.
We come to you this morning
with delight and gladness,
grateful for all of your wonders.
As the fields produce their harvest,
may your love grow within us,
that we too may produce a harvest
of love, hope, and joy. Amen.

PROCLAMATION AND RESPONSE

Prayer of Confession (James 1, Mark 7)

God of justice and righteousness,
your call beckons to us:
to live faithful lives,
to turn from wickedness,
to walk in your ways;
yet it is so easy to turn aside:
to speak a thoughtless word,
to ignore those in need,
to strike out in anger,
to forget your ways.
Forgive us.
Implant your word in our hearts,
and cleanse us from all evil.

By the power of your love,
 save our souls,
 that we might faithfully serve you. Amen.

Words of Assurance (Psalm 45, James 1)
God's word has the power to save your soul.
God has anointed you with gladness.
You are forgiven to live in joy.

Passing the Peace of Christ (James 1)
You are God's beloved children. Look into one another's
face to see the beauty of God's presence. Share the Lord's
peace with gladness.

Response to the Word (Song of Solomon 2, Mark 7)
God of abundant love,
 you delight us with your grace—
  grace expressed in the beauty of our world.
God of truth and light,
 you challenge us to live faithful lives—
  to turn away from evil,
  to follow your ways,
  to serve your people.
May your word of truth grow within us this day,
 that we may bring forth a harvest of peace. Amen.

THANKSGIVING AND COMMUNION

Invitation to the Offering (James 1)
Every generous act of giving, as with every perfect gift, is
from above. May God's word of truth, implanted within
us at birth, bloom in acts of loving faithfulness. May that
word shape our lives so that we become doers of the
word, using God's gifts for all.

Offering Prayer (James 1)
God of light and beauty,
 every gift is from you.
Even our ability to give
 is a blessing of your love.

We offer you what we have
and what we are.
Use our gifts
to give birth to a world of righteousness
where none are in need
and where all draw close to your grace.
Amen.

SENDING FORTH

Benediction (Song of Solomon 2, Psalm 45, James 1)
Arise, my fair ones, and come away.
Go forth in joy to serve with love.
Be doers of God's word.
God has blessed you forever!

CONTEMPORARY OPTIONS

Contemporary Gathering Words (Song of Solomon 2, Psalm 45)
Arise, my fair ones, and come away!
Where are we going?
We go to the realm of God's love,
a place of great beauty.
What will we find?
We will find music and sweetness,
an abundance of grace.
We come with joy to meet our Lord!

Praise Sentences (Psalm 45)
Our hearts overflow with love for you!
You have blessed us with gladness beyond compare!
Your goodness endures forever!
We rejoice in your love!

SEPTEMBER 6, 2009

Fourteenth Sunday after Pentecost
_____

Jennifer Yocum

COLOR
Green

SCRIPTURE READINGS
Proverbs 22:1-2, 8-9, 22-23; Psalm 125 (or Psalm 124); James 2:1-10 (11-13) 14-17; Mark 7:24-37

THEME IDEAS
The creation and experience of poverty comes from a systemic addiction to scarcity. The idea that there is not enough food or grace or medicine to go around is an illusion that points to the absence of faith. In many ways, Jesus' command to the deaf man to "be opened" is a commandment to our own closed hearts.

INVITATION AND GATHERING

Call to Worship (Proverbs 22)
All who have ears to hear, hearken to God's voice.
Whoever sows injustice will reap calamity.
Whoever wields the rod of anger will suffer failure.
Those who are generous are blessed,
for they share their bread with the poor.
The rich and the poor have this in common:
the Lord is the maker of them all.

Let us sing praises to the Lord
who bestows blessings on us all.

Opening Prayer (Labor Day)

Holy One,
on this Labor Day weekend
we remember the struggles and victories
of workers who found their voice
in the power of community.
Lord God,
you call us to labor together
to create more justice in this world.
May this Labor Day celebration
inspire us with the courage
of our foremothers and forefathers
to come together in hope,
sacrifice, and unity. Amen.

PROCLAMATION AND RESPONSE

Prayer of Confession (Mark 7)

Dear God,
too many of our days are consumed with doubt—
doubt if there is enough love, enough blessing,
enough creativity, enough grace, enough compass-
sion, or enough kindness in the world
to bring about the promise of your kingdom.
Dear God,
we wonder if even your great love
can make a difference in our lives.
Convinced of our unworthiness,
our hearts and our imaginations
wither and harden in despair,
as we turn away from you.
Shatter the illusions
that separate us from each other.
Pour out your life-giving waters

on our wounded hearts
in forgiveness and grace.

Words of Assurance (Mark 7)
Our God is always ready
to rain blessings on us,
to pour hope into our souls.
By the life and love of Jesus the Christ,
we are redeemed in God's eyes.

Passing the Peace of Christ
In the joy of knowing that our forgiveness is assured, turn
to one another and pass the peace of Christ.

Response to the Word (Mark 7, James 2)
Holy One,
you remind us
that wisdom may be found
in every face, every situation, every person.
God, help us erase our fears
of those who are rich or poor.
Help us see past
our cultural prejudices and assumptions.
Help our ears and our hearts
be open to your teachings. Amen.

THANKSGIVING AND COMMUNION

Invitation to the Offering (James 2)
May the God who provides us with everything we need
grant us the gift of God's own generosity as we make our
offerings today. Amen.

Offering Prayer (James 2)
God of abundant love,
bless this offering and guide its use,
that we may bring love, justice, hope,
and freedom in our world. Amen.

Invitation to Communion (Mark 7)
We are not dogs fighting over scraps,
but God's own beloved people.

The feast laid before us today has no price,
  but is freely offered by the one
    who gave us everything,
      including his life.
In freedom, in community,
  in trust of God's abundance
    for every good thing in this life,
      we are invited to take our place at this table.
Come, for all is ready.

Great Thanksgiving (James 2)
Nourished by your word and revitalized by your grace,
  we offer thanks to you, O God.
Transformed by your blessings,
  we ask to become blessings for our larger community.
May the peace, connection, and love we feel this morning
  last through tomorrow afternoon
    and through every evening and morning this week
      until we come back together in worship. Amen.

SENDING FORTH

Benediction (James 2, Mark 7)
God of rich and poor,
  God of stranger and friend,
    your love has no limits,
    your grace has no end.
Whether we see ourselves as rich or poor,
  stranger or friend,
    help us carry the good news
      of your everlasting love
        into our world. Amen.

CONTEMPORARY OPTIONS

Contemporary Gathering Words (James 2, Mark 7)
Some days we are rich, and some days poor ...
  God, remind us that you love us as we are.
Some days we are strangers, and some days friends ...

God, remind us to love each other as we are.
Some days we are blind and deaf, some days able
to see and hear everything ...
**God, remind us to keep our eyes and ears
turned to you.**

Praise Sentences
Blessed be the God who loves us no matter what!
Blessed be the God who loves us no matter what!

SEPTEMBER 13, 2009

Fifteenth Sunday after Pentecost
Mary J. Scifres

COLOR
Green

SCRIPTURE READINGS
Proverbs 1:20-33; Psalm 19; James 3:1-12; Mark 8:27-38

THEME IDEAS
The truth of God's wisdom is beautiful and life-giving. When we neglect this truth, we are lost, walking on paths that lead to death and confusion. When, with the same tongues we use to "bless" our God, we curse this truth by cursing others, we invite anguish and distress to be our companions. But when we live in this truth our souls are revived and our lives are restored. When we heed God's commandments the path is clear and joy is the reward.

INVITATION AND GATHERING

Call to Worship (Proverbs 1, Psalm 19, Mark 8)
Wisdom cries in the street, calling aloud to each of us.
  Hear her voice, and walk in God's ways.
Wisdom speaks of God's truth, proclaiming God's praise.
  Heed her counsel, and follow the Lord.

—Or—

Call to Worship (Psalm 19, Mark 8)

The heavens are singing, proclaiming God's creation.
Glory to God, and praise to God's name!
God's law is perfect; God's teachings are sure.
Rejoice, O heart; be revived, O soul!
Christ's way is clear; the way is right.
May we follow God's path, and live in Christ's light!

Opening Prayer (Proverbs 1, Psalm 19, Mark 8)

God of wisdom and truth,
　　speak to us now.
Inspire us with your word.
Speak clearly to our hearts,
　　that we may walk in your ways
　　　　and live in your love.
In the name of Christ, our Messiah,
　　we pray. Amen.

PROCLAMATION AND RESPONSE

Prayer of Confession (Proverbs 1, Psalm 19, James 3)

Wise, knowing God,
　　you see our hearts so clearly.
You speak to our lives so profoundly.
And yet, we are often unable or unwilling
　　to hear your truth
　　　　and go where you lead.
Even as we praise you with our mouths,
　　we disgrace ourselves
　　　　in words spoken to others
　　　　　　with tongues of vicious fire.
Forgive us for our hard hearts
　　and stubborn ears.
Forgive us for our hateful words
　　and cruel gossip.
Forgive us for our willful ignorance
　　of the joy and gift you offer
　　　　in your law of love.

Help us live in your love
    and walk in your truth,
        that we might be your people,
           and you might be our God.
In Christ's name, we pray. Amen.

Words of Assurance (Proverbs 1)

Those who listen to God's wisdom
    live secure and at peace,
        without dread of disaster.
Christ is our wisdom and our way.
In Christ, we are forgiven!

Passing the Peace of Christ (James 3)

As forgiven and reconciled people of God, let us greet one another with words of peace and love.

Invitation to the Word (Proverbs 1)

Wisdom cries out in God's holy word.
    **Speak to us, O Truth, that we may know
    your teachings.**
Wisdom raises her voice and calls to us now.
    **Pour out your thoughts, God of love and life,
    that we may walk in your ways.**

—Or—

Preparing to Hear the Word (Psalm 19)

May the words of our mouths and the meditations of our hearts be acceptable to you, O God, our Rock and our Redeemer.

Response to the Word or Benediction (Psalm 19)

The heavens tell of your glory, O God.
    May our lives tell the story of your grace!
The earth proclaims your creative power, mighty one.
    May our actions proclaim your amazing love!

THANKSGIVING AND COMMUNION

Invitation to the Offering or Invitation to Communion (Psalm 19)

Come to the table. Let our gifts be God's praise. As we are fed by God's mercy and grace, let us share from our abundance, that others may be fed and nourished by our love and our care.

Offering Prayer (Psalm 19)

Glorious God,
   your teachings are more to be desired
     than gold or silver.
May these gifts be transformed
   into your gifts
     for all the world.
May our lives drip
   with the sweetness of your truth.
May our love flow
   with the honey of your grace.
Bless these gifts and bless our lives,
   that all may glorify you.
In trust, we pray. Amen.

SENDING FORTH

Benediction (Psalm 19, Mark 8)

May the words of our mouths be acceptable and true.
May the meditations of our hearts be loving and pure.
May the actions of our lives be grace-filled and kind.
May we go where Christ leads and walk in God's truth.

CONTEMPORARY OPTIONS

Contemporary Gathering Words (Proverbs 1, Psalm 19)

Come, hear of God's wisdom.
Come, drink of Christ's truth.
Come, breathe the Spirit of love.
Come, walk in the way of the Lord.

Praise Sentences (Psalm 19)
The heavens are singing.
God's glory be praised!
The earth is proclaiming.
God's glory be praised!

SEPTEMBER 20, 2009

Sixteenth Sunday after Pentecost
Rebecca J. Kruger Gaudino

COLOR
Green

SCRIPTURE READINGS
Proverbs 31:10-31; Psalm 1; James 3:13–4:3, 7-8a; Mark 9:30-37

THEME IDEAS
This Sunday's texts speak about a way of seeing and interacting with the world—a way that comes from God. Each text bids us seek this divine perspective in our human lives. Recent scholarship on the Proverbs text links the "good wife" (better translated "woman of strength") with Woman Wisdom (Proverbs 1–9). Choose as your partner in life, Proverbs advises, the Wisdom of God, for only she can bring you a life of security, honor, and mercy. While the previous chapters of Proverbs have instructed us how to find this partner, Psalm 1 (a Wisdom psalm), puts it all in a nutshell: seek God and meditate on God's ordering of the world. James continues this look at wisdom, speaking of this gift as something that comes "from above" and bears "good fruits" in our lives. While Proverbs and Psalm 1 speak of the prosperity that wisdom can bring us, Jesus and James remind us that to embrace

this divine perspective is to put aside the usual definitions of success and honor.

INVITATION AND GATHERING

Call to Worship (Proverbs 31, Psalm 1, James 3)
Who is wise and understanding among us?
**Those who seek wisdom and understanding
each and every day. Those who delight in God
and meditate on God's law.**
Come, learn more about the wisdom from above,
a wisdom that yields a harvest of righteousness.
**O God, your wisdom is more precious than jewels!
We draw near to you.**

Opening Prayer (Psalm 1, James 3)
We draw near to you, O God,
Source of all understanding,
and ask you to draw near to us.
Teach us your wisdom from above,
that we may bear good fruit in our lives.
Root us beside the streams of your wisdom,
that the green leaves of our goodness,
fed by your insight,
may not wither. Amen.

PROCLAMATION AND RESPONSE

Prayer of Confession (James 3)
O God,
we live our lives as best we can—
dealing with difficult relationships and situations,
putting failures and disappointments behind us,
and moving into each new day
with as much energy, goodwill,
and optimism as we can muster.
But here, right now,
we seldom have the right answers,
we seldom seek your higher wisdom in our lives,

we just move ahead.
Forgive us for not asking for your insight.
Fill us with your wisdom,
    that we may live lives
        of goodness and peace. Amen.

Words of Assurance (James 3)

When we come before God in humility and honesty,
    God draws near to us with forgiveness
        and renewed blessing.
Thanks be to God!

Passing the Peace of Christ (James 3)

Jesus came to bring peace among us. Let us sow the seeds
for peace in our world by sharing the peace of Christ with
one another, stranger and friend alike.

Response to the Word (Proverbs 31, Psalm 1, James 3, Mark 9)

We ask for your wisdom, O God,
    not the earthly wisdom
        that we hear and see every day.
Let your understanding
    flow through our lives like a stream,
        so that we may bear the good fruits
            of welcome and compassion.
Teach us that our true dignity
    is found in honoring you
        by serving others. Amen.

THANKSGIVING AND COMMUNION

Invitation to the Offering (Proverbs 31:20, Mark 9, James 3)

The writer of Proverbs teaches that God's Wisdom is present and active in our lives in this way: "She opens her
hand to the poor, / and reaches out her hands to the
needy." Jesus lived this wisdom in his life, and called his
disciples to this same generosity. Let us give out of this
same generous wisdom—a wisdom that seeks a presence
and purpose in our lives on behalf of all.

Offering Prayer (James 3)

You are the generous one,
   full of mercy
      and goodness for your creation.
Send your wisdom with these gifts,
   that they may reach those
      who need your love and welcome.
Bring about a harvest of goodness
   through these gifts sown in peace. Amen.

SENDING FORTH

Benediction (Psalm 1)

We are planted by the streams of God's wisdom.
   We meditate on the desires of God,
   taking delight in the laws of God.
Sink your roots deep into the soil,
and draw on God's wisdom.
   For God will nourish us every day with insight.
Go forth, knowing that God watches over you.

CONTEMPORARY OPTIONS

Contemporary Gathering Words (James 3)

Are you longing for more wisdom in your life?
Do you face conflicts that need answers,
   tough situations that require special insight?
Do you need more peace in your life?
Do you long to bear good fruit in your life?
Draw near to God, the giver of wisdom,
   and God will draw near to you.

Praise Sentences

Your wisdom is great, O God.
   Teach us your ways.
Your wisdom brings life, O Lord.
   Teach us your ways.
Teach us your ways, O Lord.
   Teach us your ways.
(B. J. Beu)

SEPTEMBER 27, 2009

Seventeenth Sunday after Pentecost
Mary J. Scifres

COLOR

Green

SCRIPTURE READINGS

Esther 7:1-6, 9-10; 9:20-22; Psalm 124; James 5:13-20; Mark 9:38-50

THEME IDEAS

Service and prayer are two of the greatest gifts we give to one another and to the world. Today's New Testament readings point to the power and privilege we have as humans in partnership with God to make this world a better place. Whether casting out demons or sharing a cup of water, gifts of healing and service in Christ's name are blessed gifts to God and to God's world. Whether praying or praising, the Christian community has great power when it calls upon God's name. Even Esther saw the power she could wield when moving forward in faith. Lest we fall into sin, we would do well to remember the power God offers to and through us and to use it carefully and caringly.

INVITATION AND GATHERING

Call to Worship (Psalm 124, James 5)

Blessed be the Lord, the maker of heaven and earth!
Praise be to God, the Giver of many gifts!
Our help is in God's name, the One who calls us here.
**We come with songs of praise, with prayers
too deep for words.**
Blessed be the Lord, the maker of heaven and earth!
Blessed be the Lord!

Opening Prayer (James 5, Mark 9)

Christ Jesus,
    we come into your presence
        from many different places.
We come with songs of joy
    and shouts of gratitude.
We come carrying heavy burdens
    and sighs of suffering.
As you welcome us into your house,
    lift our burdens
        and receive our praise.
Salt us with your grace
    and flavor us with your mercy.
Bind us together,
    that we may be at peace with one another
        and be strengthened to go forth
            in service to the world.
In your holy name, we pray. Amen.

PROCLAMATION AND RESPONSE

Call to Confession (James 5)

The prayer of the faithful is strong and powerful, bringing
forgiveness of sins. Let us confess our sins to one another
and before our God, that we may be healed and forgiven.

Prayer of Confession (James 5, Mark 9)

God of unity,
    we do not always live as people

bound together in your love.
Forgive us, Holy One:
    when we do not pray for those who suffer,
        or care for those who are sick;
    when we forget to offer words of gratitude
        for the many gifts in our lives;
    when we judge others and neglect your teaching
        that we are in partnership with one another;
    when we lose the saltiness of your teachings,
        the excitement and energy you offer us
            on this journey of discipleship.
Flavor us with your love.
Knead into our very being
    your mercy and your grace.
Sprinkle us with the spices
    of compassion and commitment.
Even as we are forgiven,
    leaven us with forgiveness for others.
In trust of your eternal grace
    and merciful forgiveness, we pray. Amen.

Words of Assurance (James 5:15)

Scripture promises:
    "Anyone who has committed sins will be forgiven."
Friends, no matter how great our sins,
    or how far we have wandered from the path,
        the word of scripture is true.
In the name of Christ, in Christ's mercy and love,
    we are all forgiven and reconciled to God.

Passing the Peace of Christ (Mark 9:50)

Christ calls to us, "Be at peace with one another." Let us
turn to our neighbor and offer signs of the peace and love
to which we are called.

THANKSGIVING AND COMMUNION

Call to Prayer (James 5)

Are any among us suffering? Let us offer prayers for healing. Are any among us cheerful? Let us offer words of

praise. Come! Let us pray together, for the prayer of the righteous is powerful.

Prayers of the People (James 5, Mark 9)

(Any person may offer a brief spoken prayer or lift a name following each petition. The unison response may follow individual prayers or the group of prayers.)

God of love and power, hear our prayers
 as we raise our thoughts and our voices to you.
We pray for those who suffer and are sick ...
God of love and power,
 hear our prayer.
We pray for those who struggle with temptation and sin ...
God of love and power,
 hear our prayer.
We pray for those who lead and guide others
 on the journey of faith ...
God of love and power,
 hear our prayer.
We pray for those who serve and share in ministry
 around the world ...
God of love and power,
 hear our prayer.
We pray for the world and its leaders ...
God of love and power,
 hear our prayer.
We give thanks for those who are cheerful
 and who bring joy to our lives ...
God of love and power,
 we give you praise.
We give thanks for those who are loving and kind ...
God of love and power,
 we give you praise.
We give thanks for those who serve and lead us
 in our journeys of faith ...
God of love and power,
 we give you praise.
We give thanks for this earth and its bounty ...
God of love and power,

we give you praise.
We give thanks for Christ's grace in our lives,
    and for the presence of God in our world ...
God of love and power,
    we give you praise.
God of love and power, hear our prayers
    as we raise our thoughts and our voices to you. Amen.

SENDING FORTH

Benediction (Mark 9)
You are the light of the world!
Let your light shine for all to see!
You are the salt of the earth!
Let your salt flavor this earth with God's love!
Go forth as salt and light.
Be at peace with God's amazing world.

CONTEMPORARY OPTIONS

Contemporary Gathering Words (James 5, Mark 9)
Come, you who are suffering and sick.
    God is our help and our strength.
Come, you who are filled with joy.
    God is our help and our strength.
Come, people of faith, your prayers are needed here.
    God is our help and our strength.
Come, saints and sinners alike.
    God is our help and our strength.
Come, sprinkled with salt or dull with doubt.
    God is our help and our strength.
Come, call on Christ's name and trust in God's love.
    God is our help and our strength.

Praise Sentences (Psalm 124)
Blessed be the Lord!
    Bless God's holy name!
Blessed be the Lord!
    Bless God's holy name!

OCTOBER 4, 2009

Eighteenth Sunday after Pentecost/
World Communion Sunday

B. J. Beu

COLOR
Green

SCRIPTURE READINGS
Job 1:1; 2:1-10; Psalm 26 (or Psalm 25); Hebrews 1:1-4; 2:5-12; Mark 10:2-16

THEME IDEAS
The readings from Job and Psalm 26 are a celebration of personal integrity in faith. God boasts of Job's integrity, proclaiming him a blameless and upright man, even after Satan was allowed to devastate his family and livelihood—even his health. Job illustrates that suffering is no indicator of whether one has lived a godly life. The psalmist brags of personal integrity, challenging God (foolishly, in light of Job) to put this integrity to the test. The Hebrews reading could be used to speak of Christ's integrity and how he was made higher than the angels because of his faithfulness. The gospel reading does not fit with the other texts and deals with marriage, divorce, adultery, and entering the kingdom of God like children.

INVITATION AND GATHERING

Call to Worship (Job 1–2, Psalm 26)
In this world of hardship and pain,
walk with integrity before the Lord.
Save us from the time of trial, O God.
The pious lose their jobs and their livelihoods.
The righteous are struck down with disease and death.
Save us from the time of trial, O God.
Families are swallowed up in war.
Children are beaten and sold into slavery.
Save us from the time of trial, O God.
Shall we receive the good at the hand of God,
and not receive the bad?
**In this world of hardship and pain,
we will walk with integrity before the Lord.**

Opening Prayer (Hebrews 1, Mark 10)
Eternal God,
long ago you spoke to our ancestors
in many and various ways by the prophets;
but in these last days, you have spoken to us
by a Son.
May we become again like children
and receive your kingdom in our midst,
that we may walk in your ways without faltering,
and trust in your Spirit without wavering. Amen.

PROCLAMATION AND RESPONSE

Prayer of Confession (Job 1–2, Psalm 26)
Holy God,
it is easy to boast of our faithfulness
when life is easy
and your blessings cascade over us
like ever-flowing streams.
Stop our mouths
when we brag of our integrity

and deride others
for their wayward feet.
Help us be more like Jesus,
who taught his disciples to pray
that they may be spared
from the time of trial,
than like the psalmist, who challenged:
"Prove me, O LORD, and try me;
test my heart and mind."
May our faithfulness
speak louder than our words,
that others may see in our example
the joys of upright living,
whether we are receiving
the good from your hand,
or the bad. Amen.

Words of Assurance (Hebrews 2:11-12)

Hear these words from the book of Hebrews:
"The one who sanctifies and those who are sanctified all have one Father. For this reason Jesus is not ashamed to call them brothers and sisters, saying, 'I will proclaim your name to my brothers and sisters, in the midst of the congregation I will praise you.'"

Invitation to the Word (Hebrews 1–2)

Long ago, God spoke to our ancestors through the prophets. Today, God speaks to us through a Son, who is the very Word of God. As we hear the words of the prophets, may we listen for the teachings of the incarnate Word that sanctifies us through God's love.

Call to Prayer (Job 1–2, Psalm 26)

When Job's wife derided his faithfulness by saying, "Do you still persist in your integrity? Curse God, and die," Job responded, "Shall we receive the good at the hand of God, and not receive the bad?" As we come before God in prayer, may we too accept the bad with the good and keep our integrity, walking with God in trust and in unwavering faith.

THANKSGIVING AND COMMUNION

Invitation to Communion (World Communion Sunday)

Come to the table, you who are scattered and torn.
Here we find hope.
Come to the table, you who are scared and lonely.
Here we find love.
Come to the table, you who are tired and tense.
Here we find rest for our souls,
and food for our journey.
Come to the table, you who are lost and are searching.
Here we discover guidance,
and light for our darkness.
Come to the table, you who are happy or sad.
Here our lives are embraced by God's grace.
(Joanne Brown)

Great Thanksgiving

We give you thanks, our creator and liberator,
for by your word you have called forth creation,
you have created us in your image.
You led us from slavery to freedom,
going ever before us with cloud and fiery pillar.
With burning coals you gave utterance to the prophets,
demanding that justice roll down like waters,
and righteousness like an ever-flowing stream.
In the fullness of time,
your Spirit descended like a dove upon Jesus,
anointing him to preach good news to the poor,
to proclaim release to the captives
and recovery of sight to the blind,
to set at liberty those who were oppressed,
and to declare the reign of God in our midst.
When Jesus gathered together with his beloved disciples,
he was known to them in the breaking of bread.
Before feeding the multitudes,
he broke bread and gave thanks.
When two or three were gathered together,

he broke bread and gave thanks.
He sought the outcasts and broke bread with them,
    witnessing the fullness of your grace.
(Joanne Brown)

Words of Institution

On the night of his greatest trial,
    he gathered his friends together in an upper room,
        and said to them:
"Tonight I am going to create
    a sustaining community among you.
It will not require you to always be faithful or perfect
    or good or right or powerful or unblemished or pure.
It will not require you to hold an advanced degree,
    or to have the proper wealth, skin color, sexual identity,
        gender, or religion.
This community we are creating together tonight
    requires two things:
        your willingness to share with one another
        and your remembrance of me.
These two are enough to bind you to one another
    and to your work on behalf of the world.
Take this bread, the bread of life.
It represents my physical presence,
    which has been with you on many adventures.
It also represents the bodies
    of all who have tried to love mercy, create justice,
        and build the kingdom of God on earth.
Whenever you eat bread, remember this evening.
Think on what we have tried to do for the poor
    and those who are marginalized.
Take this cup, the cup of salvation.
It represents the covenant we make with each other
    to always be there for one another.
It also represents my promise to be with you always.
This cup and your thoughts of me will sustain you
    and restore your spirits."
As we break bread and drink this cup,

we do so remembering a life lived in thanksgiving—
    a life of uncompromising commitment
        to justice and equality;
    a life that led to an unjust death on a cross.
And in the darkness of night,
    when evil and betrayal seemed victorious,
    your creative power burst upon us
        in the glory of the resurrection.
In remembering all he did and taught,
    we actively await with hope
    for the coming of God's reign
        to bring peace and justice.
God of love,
    send your Holy Spirit upon us.
Bless what we do here this morning,
    that we and these gifts,
        touched by your Spirit,
        may be signs of life and love
            to each other and to all the world. Amen.
Take and eat. May you never cease to hunger for justice.
Take and drink. May you never cease to thirst for mercy.

Offering Prayer (Job 1–2)
God of whirlwind and fire,
    your ways are not our ways,
    your judgments are as high above us
        as the stars are above the sea.
We gratefully receive the blessings of your hands,
    but fear to receive the evils that befall
        our sisters and brothers.
Open our hearts
    to accept the hardships of this life
        and to rejoice in the blessings we have received,
        that we may share them with those in need.
    Amen.

SENDING FORTH

Benediction (Psalm 26, Hebrews 1–2)
Through the love of a savior,
 we are sanctified as people of God.
Through God's mercy, love, and grace,
 we are brothers and sisters with Christ.
Through the Spirit that animates our lives,
 we are the imprint of God's very being.
Go and lead lives of integrity.
Go with the blessing of Christ's love!

—Or—

Benediction (World Communion Sunday)
Ever-loving and ever-present God,
you have refreshed us at your table,
 by granting us the presence of Jesus.
May the sharing of this sacred meal together
remain always in our hearts,
 and weave us together as one body, one people.
Strengthen our faith,
that we might accomplish great things
 through our love for one another.
Send us forth into the world
in courage and peace,
 rejoicing in the power of your Holy Spirit. Amen.
(Joanne Brown and B. J. Beu)

CONTEMPORARY OPTIONS

Contemporary Gathering Words (Job 1–2)
Job was an upright man, blameless before God.
 Why then was he stricken?
God's ways are hard to understand.
 But God loved him still?
God loved Job.

Why then was he stricken?
God's ways are hard to understand.
May we be as faithful as Job
when evil befalls us.

Praise Sentences (Hebrews 1–2)

Jesus reflects God's glory.
Jesus sustains all things by his power.
Jesus is the pioneer of our salvation.
Jesus reflects God's glory.
Jesus sustains all things by his power.

OCTOBER 11, 2009

Nineteenth Sunday after Pentecost
Shelley Cunningham

COLOR

Green

SCRIPTURE READINGS

Job 23:1-9, 16-17; Psalm 22:1-15; Hebrews 4:12-16; Mark 10:17-31

THEME IDEAS

Psalm 22 is so commonly associated with Jesus' torment on Good Friday that it seems unworthy to be applied to our own lives. Yet, the psalm speaks of the suffering and emptiness that so many feel in times of unimaginable sorrow—the death of a child, the devastation of a hurricane, the anguish of a loved one away at war. There is power in acknowledging this suffering and the church's response to it. We are not called to explain life's hardships; rather, like Job, we are called to seek God's presence with us in their midst. The Hebrews text reassures us that Jesus is with us in times of trial because he himself endured such trials for our sake. Mark reminds us that when we question God's intentions for us, it is often our own choices that turn us away from God—choosing money, family, or security over God's will for our lives.

INVITATION AND GATHERING

Call to Worship (Hebrews 4, Mark 10)

The kingdom of God is at hand.
We want to enter this kingdom.
The mercy of God is made known.
We want to receive this mercy.
The grace of God is abundant for all.
**We praise you, O God, for your compassion
and your love. Accept our grateful praise
as we come to worship you today.**

Opening Prayer (Job 23, Hebrews 4)

Almighty God,
we long to rest
in your gentle arms.
We need your compassion
as we face the challenges
and disappointments of life.
When our hearts are hard,
and our concern is only for ourselves,
turn us back to you.
Remind us of your saving love
and keep us close to you, Lord.
Love us as only you can love,
in Jesus' name. Amen.

PROCLAMATION AND RESPONSE

Prayer of Confession (Psalm 22, Job 23, Mark 10)

Lord,
we look for you
in the wrong places.
We put our trust
in material things.
We worry about things
we cannot change.
We wonder

if you are even there at all.
For all the times
we have doubted you, Lord,
forgive us.
For all the ways
we have neglected your word
and ignored your people,
forgive us.
Do not be far from us, Lord.
There is no one else
we can turn to for help.
Renew our fickle hearts
and help us put our trust in you.

Words of Assurance (Psalm 22, Hebrews 4)
There is no wrong
that God cannot make right.
There is no chasm
that can separate us
from God's love.
The Lord is patient and kind,
generous and good.
God will not forsake you
or leave you.
Turn to the Lord with confidence
and put your faith in God's great mercy.
By the power of Jesus Christ,
we are made whole. Amen.

Passing the Peace of Christ (Mark 10)
In Christ we are mothers and fathers and brothers and sisters to one another. As members of God's family, let us share God's peace with one another.

Response to the Word (Job 23, Hebrews 4)
Mighty Lord,
help us look for you
in the north and in the south,
in our homes and in our workplaces,

in our families and in our relationships.
May we never stop pursuing your truth.
Assure us with your word
    that you are with us wherever we go,
        in Jesus' name. Amen.

THANKSGIVING AND COMMUNION

Invitation to Communion (Mark 10)

In this meal, Christ fills the hungry. All are welcome—rich and poor, old and young, healthy and sick. You, who long to taste heaven's goodness, come. Come to our Lord's table and be fed.

Offering Prayer (Mark 10)

With open hands and thankful hearts,
    we offer to you all that is already yours, O Lord.
Everything we possess is a gift from you.
You so freely give us what we need,
    and you promise even greater treasures
        that await us in heaven.
Take what we offer
    and use it for the goodness of your kingdom.
Help us share generously with others
    all that you so graciously give to us. Amen.

SENDING FORTH

Benediction (Mark 10, Hebrews 4)

With God all things are possible.
May you carry that confidence
    into your daily life and work,
        as you walk in Christ's footsteps,
        guided by God's hand.

CONTEMPORARY OPTIONS

Contemporary Gathering Words (Hebrews 4)

In God's mercy, we are rich.
In Jesus' love, we are welcomed.

In the Spirit's peace, we are satisfied.
Come; let us worship our savior and our king!

Praise Sentences (Mark 10)

With you, O Lord, all things are possible.
We bless you and praise your name forever.
In you, O Lord, we find our home.
We bless you and praise your name forever.
Through you, O Lord, we are made one in Christ.
We bless you and praise you, O Christ,
for your saving love.

OCTOBER 18, 2009

Twentieth Sunday after Pentecost

Mary J. Scifres

COLOR

Green

SCRIPTURE READINGS

Job 38:1-7 (34-41); Psalm 104:1-9, 24, 35c; Hebrews 5:1-10; Mark 10:35-45

THEME IDEAS

Greatness in God's eyes is quite different from greatness in the eyes of the world. To sit at Christ's right hand is to hang with thieves, to dine with sinners, to serve tirelessly. Indeed, to drink the cup that Jesus drank and to be baptized with martyrdom and death is not something for which most of us yearn. Yet, many do yearn to follow in Christ's steps, to serve with generosity, to live with kindness, to walk with humility, to care with compassion, and to be a servant to God's purpose in our lives. This yearning draws us to Christ's side and clothes us with the greatest glory of all ... the glory of love.

INVITATION AND GATHERING

Call to Worship (Psalm 104)
Look at the heavens, stretched out like a tent!
Listen to the winds, the messengers of God.

Gaze at autumn's changing colors, painted for us.
Reflect on God's mountains, majestic and strong.
Blessing and honor to our Creator God!
Majesty and praise to the One who gives us life!

Opening Prayer (Psalm 104, Mark 10)

God of majesty and might,
blow through this place
like a mighty wind.
Inspire us with your presence.
Cover us with your love,
that we might be your people,
serving others with care and compassion.
In Christ's name, we pray. Amen.

PROCLAMATION AND RESPONSE

Prayer of Confession (Mark 10)

We pray for forgiveness this day.
For choosing power over service,
forgive us.
For seeking glory rather than humility,
forgive us.
For pushing ourselves to the front,
when our presence is needed on the sidelines,
forgive us.
Help us know where we are needed
and how best to serve you and your people.
Guide us to your side,
that we might be your hands
of healing and compassion
for a world in need.
In Christ's name, we pray. Amen.

Words of Assurance (Mark 10)

Christ, our High Priest,
guides us gently back to the path—
the path of walking with God
and serving our neighbor.

In the name of Christ,
    we are forgiven!
We will be with God in paradise!

Passing the Peace of Christ
As forgiven and reconciled children of God, let us share
with one another signs of peace and love.

Response to the Word (Mark 10)
Gracious God,
    guide us into your service.
Lead us to paths of humility and compassion.
Help us remember that true greatness
    is nothing less than love
        and nothing more than servanthood.
In the name of the master who serves us best,
    Christ Jesus, we pray. Amen.

THANKSGIVING AND COMMUNION

Invitation to the Offering (Psalm 104, Mark 10)
This earth has been given to us by God, our creator. The
gifts of our lives are blessings to be shared. Let us share
our gifts as we reflect on the ways in which we can serve
and care for others and for this earth.

Offering Prayer (Psalm 104, Mark 10)
God of glory,
    we thank you for this season of abundance.
We praise you for the gifts of this earth
    and of our lives.
As we return a portion of these gifts,
    we also dedicate our lives to your service.
Bless our gifts and our service,
    that we may glorify you
        and reflect your love in all that we say
        and in all that we do. Amen.

SENDING FORTH

Benediction (Mark 10)
Go forth with care and compassion.
Go forth to serve and to love.
Go forth as children of God!

CONTEMPORARY OPTIONS

Contemporary Gathering Words (Psalm 104, Mark 10)
Come into God's presence and shout with the heavens,
our God is very great!
Clothed with honor and wrapped in glorious light,
our God is very great!
Serving tirelessly and caring endlessly,
our God is very great!
Calling us to humility and compassion,
our God is very great!
Come into God's presence, to listen and hear God speak.

Praise Sentences (Psalm 104)
Bless the Lord, O my soul!
Bless and praise the Lord!
Bless the Lord, O my soul!
Bless and praise the Lord!

OCTOBER 25, 2009

Twenty-first Sunday after Pentecost/Reformation Sunday

B. J. Beu

COLOR

Green

SCRIPTURE READINGS

Job 42:1-6, 10-17; Psalm 34:1-8 (19-22); Hebrews 7:23-28;
Mark 10:46-52

THEME IDEAS

Job and Psalm 34 present problems for preachers and worship leaders alike. While the psalmist insists that God
spares and protects the righteous, Job is a chilling example of the evil that God can bring upon anyone. The author of Job paints Job's vindication and the restoration of
Job's fortunes as of greater value than what Job lost in
God's test of his faithfulness. But can anything remotely
make up for the loss of one's family—much less to a test
of faith? If these texts are used, they must not be sugar-
coated; their full cognitive dissonance must be allowed to
play out—for such is the experience of real life. The gospel
reading adds a wonderful avenue for reflection. Blind Bartimaeus is offered the brass ring—Jesus offers to give him
anything he asks for. Not surprisingly, Bartimaeus asks
for the return of his physical sight. What would Job or we
ask for? Our children back, our sight returned, or to see

with God's eyes, to have God's salvation? What do we seek, and how well do we really see?

INVITATION AND GATHERING

Call to Worship (Job 42, Psalm 34)
Magnify the Lord; exalt God's holy name.
The Lord hears the pleas of the perishing.
Magnify the Lord; exalt God's holy name.
The Lord restores the fortunes of the righteous.
Magnify the Lord; exalt God's holy name.
The Lord redeems the lives of God's servants.

Opening Prayer (Mark 10)
God, our Healer,
   give us the courage of blind Bartimaeus,
     to cry out to you
       when we are in need;
   give us the wisdom of Job,
     to know when we have overreached
     and our cause is lost;
   give us the confidence of the psalmist,
     to sing your praises
     and magnify your name.
Grant us the wisdom, O God,
   to seek from you what is of real value—
     what will truly make us well,
     what will truly make us whole,
     what will truly give us bliss. Amen.

PROCLAMATION AND RESPONSE

Prayer of Confession (Job 42, Psalm 34, Mark 10)
God of mystery and blessing,
   we speak without knowledge,
   we grasp without looking at the consequences,
   we boast without cause,
   we speak comfort without true compassion.
Forgive our ignorance,

when we look at what others have
without seeing what they have lost.
Forgive our self-absorption
when we focus on our desires
and ignore the needs of others.
May we follow the example of Bartimaeus
and cry out our need
when you draw near. Amen.

Words of Assurance (Hebrews 7)
Since Christ intercedes for us,
he is able to save everyone
who approaches God through him.
Draw near to God through Christ,
and walk blameless in God's sight.

Invitation to the Word (Mark 10)
Listen not to the crowd. Listen to your heart and make
Christ the center of your life. As today's scriptures are
read, know that Christ calls us to follow him, that we may
be made whole.

Call to Prayer (Psalm 34)
Seek the Lord and God will answer you. The Lord will deliver you from your tears. Happy are those who take
refuge in our God. Let us pray.

THANKSGIVING AND COMMUNION

Offering Prayer (Job 42, Psalm 34, Mark 10)
Mighty God,
you restore sight to the blind
and bounty to the afflicted;
you provide refuge for the lost
and freedom for the condemned.
Open our mouths to cry out our need
and open our hearts
to give from our abundance,
in Jesus' name,
the name above all names. Amen.

SENDING FORTH

Benediction (Psalm 26, Mark 10)
Taste and see that the Lord is good.
We once were broken, but now are whole.
Taste and see that the Lord is good.
We once were blind, but now we see.
Taste and see that the Lord is good.
We once were lost, but now are found.
Taste and see that the Lord is good.
We once were alone, but now are family.

CONTEMPORARY OPTIONS

Contemporary Gathering Words (Mark 10)
Jesus asks us: "What do you want from me?"
Loving savior, restore our sight.
Jesus prods us: "What do you need from me?"
Loving Guide, be our vision.
Jesus questions us: "What do you want from me?"
Loving teacher, show us how to live.

Praise Sentences (Mark 10)
The blind see.
The broken are made whole.
God has done great things for us.
Taste and see that the Lord is good.
Blessed be the Lord.

NOVEMBER 1, 2009

All Saints Day
Robert Blezard

COLOR
White

SCRIPTURE READINGS
Isaiah 25:6-9; Psalm 24; Revelation 21:1-6a; John 11:32-44

THEME IDEAS
The four lections rejoice in God's ultimate deliverance of humanity from death and worldly sorrow—appropriate themes when we remember the saints who have gone before us. Isaiah speaks of God destroying death and wiping away every tear. Revelation employs Isaiah's images in its description of a new heaven and new earth. Psalm 24 speaks of God as the reign of the sovereign of glory. Finally, John speaks of deliverance from death when Jesus raises Lazarus—wiping the tears of grief from many faces: Mary's, Martha's, the other mourners, even his own.

INVITATION AND GATHERING
Call to Worship (Isaiah 25)
Come to the banquet our God has prepared for us.
God sets a table for all the saints—
saints from all times and places.
Come! God provides abundantly for everyone.

**We will feast on the bread of life,
and the wine of salvation.**
God has removed our burial shroud
and destroyed death forever.
**God takes away our disgrace
and will wipe away our tears.**
Come to the feast! Celebrate God's love and mercy.
We are glad and rejoice in God's salvation.

Opening Prayer (John 11)

Saving God,
    in each generation
        you call your sons and daughters
            from the dark caverns of death
                into the bright light of new life.
We are grateful for the faithful witness
    of all the saints who have gone before us
        and who now rest from their labors.
As we worship today,
    roll away the stones
        that keep us trapped in darkness.
May we hear your voice calling us to new life
    and shrug off the burial cloths
        that keep us bound to sin and death.
In your name we pray, Amen.

PROCLAMATION AND RESPONSE

Prayer of Confession (Isaiah 25, John 11)

We have heard you
    calling us to life, O God,
        but are trapped in dark caverns
            of self-interest and doubt.
We have received your invitation
    to the banquet for your saints,
        but are distracted by many things—
            our hectic schedules,
            our preoccupation with the affairs of the world,

our love for ourselves,
    instead of love for you and our neighbor.
As we kneel before you,
    we ask that you renew our lives
        and wipe away our tears. Amen.

Words of Assurance (Revelation 21)

Jesus said, "I am the Alpha and the Omega,
    the beginning and the end. To the thirsty
    I will give water as a gift from the spring
    of the water of life."
In the name of the Alpha and Omega,
    your sins are forgiven.
May you be renewed by the One
    who makes all things new.

Passing the Peace of Christ (John 11, Revelation 21)

The Lord our God delivers you from death,
offering refreshment from the spring of the water of life.
May the peace of Christ be with you.
    And also with you.
Let us share signs of God's peace with one another.

Invitation to the Word (Isaiah 25, John 11)

O God, you speak to us in scripture.
You call us out of darkness
    and invite us to feed at the banquet of life,
    a smorgasbord of good things.
As you have with the saints of every age,
    prepare our ears and hearts,
    that our ears may hear your word
    and our hearts may respond with love.
    Amen. Give us ears to hear and hearts to receive.

Response to the Word (John 11)

God promises that if we believe,
    we will see God's glory.
May we, who have heard God's word, have faith,
    that we may see God's glory and live in God's light.
    Revive us, God. Unbind us and let us go free.

THANKSGIVING AND COMMUNION

Invitation to the Offering (Isaiah 25)

God provides blessings in abundance for all people, not for us alone. May we who are blessed with more than we need rejoice in our plenty and return to God a portion that may provide for the church and sustain those who live in need.

Offering Prayer (Isaiah 25)

God of plenty,
    receive these gifts of treasure
    and accept our gifts of talent and time as well.
Remind us that we can never give of our bounty
    beyond your capacity to replenish.
God of plenty,
    gather together these scraps
    that we take from our plates of plenty.
Join them with the offerings
    of all your children
        who sit at your feast.
Use our gifts according to your will,
    that they may be a blessing
        for those in need.

SENDING FORTH

Benediction (John 11)

God calls us to come to life, to leave our tombs,
    to be unbound, and to be set free.
Go, therefore, and walk in the world with confidence.
We rejoice in our new lives!
In all we do and all that we say,
    we will proclaim the one who sets us free.
Amen!

CONTEMPORARY OPTIONS

Contemporary Gathering Words (John 11)

We are the dead, trapped in our tombs,
wrapped in layers of selfishness and sin.
Roll away the stone and call us to life.
Our bindings will fall and we will be free.

—Or—

Contemporary Gathering Words (Revelation 21, Isaiah 25)

Are you thirsty?
Yes, we're thirsty for life.
Are you hungry?
Yes, we're hungry for spirituality.
Are you sad?
Yes, the world's a sad place.
Are you tired?
Yes, we are weary of the world.
Drink then, thirsty ones, from God's spring of life.
Eat then, hungry ones, from God's banquet table.
Be comforted, sad ones, for God wipes away every tear.
Be refreshed, weary ones, for God revives the spirit.
Thanks be to God! Amen!

Praise Sentences (Psalm 24, John 11, Revelation 21)

Praise the king of glory!
God prepares a feast for us!
Praise the king of glory!
God gives us living water!
Praise the king of glory!
God wipes away our tears!
Praise the king of glory!
God brings us new life!
Praise the king of glory!
God sets us free to live!
Praise the king of glory!
Praise God's mighty name!

NOVEMBER 8, 2009

Twenty-third Sunday after Pentecost
Shari Jackson Monson

COLOR
Green

SCRIPTURE READINGS
Ruth 3:1-5; 4:13-17; Psalm 127 (or Psalm 42); Hebrews 9:24-28; Mark 12:28-44

THEME IDEAS
Can you imagine coming to worship as a widow who is ready to give her last dime for the sake of the cross? Imagine the cost of her devotion. Today is about honoring the sacrifice of both the widow and her savior. Our themes from scripture include: accepting the values of God's kingdom; releasing the grasp of our culture; learning to give out of our abundance; and nourishing our souls with the hope that comes from God, through crying out in honest, searching prayer. The psalmist in particular reminds us that all human activity has no value outside of God's economy—be it the securing of housing, the protection of cities, or providing for families. We can rest in these assurances: God builds, God protects, God provides.

INVITATION AND GATHERING

Call to Worship (Psalm 42)

Our souls long for you, O God.
When shall we behold your face?
Our souls are uneasy.
When shall hope lead us to praise you again?
During the day, your steadfast love sustains us.
During the night, your song washes over us.
Our hope leads us to praise you.
We praise you, our song of hope.

Opening Prayer (Ruth 3–4, Psalm 127)

Lord,
  we come into your house
    as people seeking a heritage.
We need your provision in our lives,
  just as you provided
    for your daughter Ruth.
A foreigner without status,
  you gave her a home,
    a family, and a heritage.
Your provision is enough;
  it is all we need.
Bring us into your heritage
  and form us into your people,
    mighty God, restorer of our lives!

PROCLAMATION AND RESPONSE

Prayer of Confession (Mark 12)

Lord of all,
  the nations are yours.
The poor are your treasured ones—
  widows, orphans, the aliens you protect.
Your justice reigns over all.
Forgive us when our ways
  devour your beloved.

We don't mean to cause harm,
   yet we do.
Forgive us when we consume
   more than our fair share,
   all the while knowing
      that our excesses deny the poor
      the things they need to live.
Forgive us for building bigger closets,
   and not clothing the naked.
Forgive us for vacationing in leisure,
   when multitudes long simply for rest.
Hear our prayer, Holy One.
May your justice and grace
   reign forever. Amen.

Words of Assurance (Hebrews 9)
We long to mend our ways.
Christ can bear these sins
   for all who eagerly wait for him.
His sacrifice on our behalf,
   his grace toward us,
   washes us anew.

Passing the Peace of Christ
Family members of the risen Lord, it's time for a reunion!
Turn to your Christian brothers and sisters and pass the
peace of Christ.

Response to the Word
(Consider giving everyone a dime, today's widow's mite, at the
conclusion of the service. Remind the congregation, prior to the
benediction, of the relative "cheapness" of this token remembrance gift. In Tanzania, for example, this would purchase clean
drinking water for one day and equate to 30 percent of one's
wages. A widow's mite—it is costly to bear the truth of God's
economy.)

THANKSGIVING AND COMMUNION

Invitation to the Offering

O Lord,
  you graciously pour out your blessings on us.
Your gifts surround us.
Despite our abundance,
  help us see the widow's gift,
  for we long to give as she did,
    gladly giving all she had.
All we have
  is a gift from your hand.
Help us loosen our hands,
  giving to work of this church on your behalf,
  for in giving freely to you,
    we gain the opportunity
      to live abundant lives!

Offering Prayer or Communion Prayer or Great Thanksgiving

Take this, the gifts of our hands,
  and the enterprise of our families,
  and bless and multiply them
    for the sake of your kingdom alone. Amen.

SENDING FORTH

Benediction

To live as God's people of abundance,
  while not giving in to the pull of our culture,
  you're going to need the power
    of the Holy Spirit.
Lift your hands and hearts,
  in the name of the Father, who sustains us,
  and the Son, who instructs us,
  and the Spirit, who leads us.
Go forth to love and serve the Lord—
  the one who loves the widow and the orphan.
Sing the Lord's song of hope in dry lands!

CONTEMPORARY OPTIONS

Contemporary Gathering Words (Psalm 42)

My soul thirsts for you, O God.
Lord, be my provision.
We are without comfort and are lost.
Lord, be our guide.
Your people long to know your hope.
Lord, be our song.
We come to worship you, Lord of all!

Praise Sentences

God's love lifts us up.
God's love fills us with joy.
God's love heals our wounds.
God's love is enough.
God's love is all we'll ever need.
(B. J. Beu)

NOVEMBER 15, 2009

Twenty-fourth Sunday after Pentecost
Mary J. Scifres

COLOR

Green

SCRIPTURE READINGS

1 Samuel 1:4-20; 2:1-10 (or Psalm 113); Hebrews 10:11-14 (15-18) 19-25; Mark 13:1-8

THEME IDEAS

Today's pre-Advent readings foreshadow the prophetic warnings and hope that come with the early readings in Advent. Mary's Magnificat closely mirrors Hannah's song of praise (1 Samuel 2:1-10). Together, these women celebrate the miracle of life—springing forth, and overcoming despair and fear. Hope wins the day, as barrenness is banished and fertile ground is found (1 Samuel 1). Hope wins the day, as the hungry are fed with abundance, and the poor are raised up to seats of honor (1 Samuel 2). Hope wins the day, as sins are forgiven through Christ's grace (Hebrews 10). Hope wins the day, as Jesus becomes the cornerstone that never fails (Mark 13). Hope is the gift that sustains us through days of darkness and times of waiting.

INVITATION AND GATHERING

Call to Worship (1 Samuel 2, Mark 13)

Let our hearts rejoice in the God of hope and faithfulness.
Our strength is in the maker of heaven and earth.
Our foundation is the cornerstone that never fails.
The rock of ages is a foundation like no other.
Hope arises, as the tools of war are broken
and the weak are given strength.
**Hope lives when the hungry are fed
and the poor are lifted up.**
God comes bringing judgment to the ends of the earth,
calling us to hope and faithfulness.
Come, rock of ages, come quickly now.

Opening Prayer (1 Samuel 1)

God of possibilities,
    fill us with your hope and faithfulness.
Listen to us
    as we pour out our souls before you.
Grant us the grace to be your people
    and to live your teachings.
Live in us,
    that we may arise with hope
        and walk in love.
In the name of Christ our rock,
    we pray. Amen.

PROCLAMATION AND RESPONSE

Call to Confession (Hebrews 10)

By a single offering, Christ has perfected us for all time.
Let us approach this time of confession with true hearts,
in full assurance that Christ's mercy is strong enough to
bear all of our burdens.

Prayer of Confession (1 Samuel 1)

Merciful God,
    look upon us,

your servants gathered here,
    with grace and compassion.
Hear our every need.
Speak to our fearful hearts,
    that we may pour out our confessions
    and admit our wrongdoings.
(*Silent prayer*)
Loving God,
    you have heard our anxieties,
    our vexations, our worries,
    our hopes, our dreams.
Breathe in us the spirit of forgiveness,
    that we may receive your grace,
    and may walk in freedom
        and glorious hope.
In Christ's name, we pray. Amen.

Words of Assurance (Hebrews 10)

Hold fast to the confession of our hope without wavering,
    for our God, the God of all ages,
    the one who has promised forgiveness,
        is faithful!
In the name of Christ, you are forgiven!

Passing the Peace of Christ (Hebrews 10)

Let us share together the peace of Christ, encouraging one
another in love and goodness.

Prayers of the People (1 Samuel 2)

For leaders and those in power,
    that they might walk in your ways of love ...
    God of all hopefulness,
    remember your people.
For people who are weak and in need,
    that they might feel the strength of your compassion ...
    God of all hopefulness,
    remember your people.
For those who are hungry or poor,
    that they might find abundance in our generosity ...

God of all hopefulness,
remember your people.
For those who are downtrodden or dispirited,
that they might be lifted up with arms of hope ...
God of all hopefulness,
remember your people.
For the Church and all who call upon your name,
that we might be found faithful ...
God of all hopefulness,
remember your people.
For all who hunger and thirst for righteousness,
that your kingdom might come,
your will be done, today and forevermore ...
God of all hopefulness,
remember your people.
Amen and amen.

THANKSGIVING AND COMMUNION

Invitation to the Offering (1 Samuel 1, Hebrews 10)
Hannah offered the life of her much-awaited son, that she
might honor and glorify God. Jesus offered his very life,
that we might know God's love fully and completely. As
we offer our gifts to God, let us do so with the same generosity of spirit that has been shown to us in so many
ways.

Offering Prayer (1 Samuel 2)
God of all hopefulness,
strengthen us this day
to live in hope and gratitude.
Give us the courage
to live as people of generosity.
Multiply our gifts,
that the hungry might be fed
and the poor might find abundance.
In Christ's name, we pray. Amen.

SENDING FORTH

Benediction (Hebrews 10, Mark 13)

Go in peace, encouraging one another in love,
and looking with hope for the kingdom of God.

CONTEMPORARY OPTIONS

Contemporary Gathering Words (1 Samuel 2, Hebrews 10)

There is no holy one like God above.
There is no rock like our God.
There is no hope like the hope of God's strength for us.
There is no hope like our God.
There is no promise like the promise of Christ's mercy
and grace.
There is no promise like our God.
There is no love as great as the love God offers today
and all days.
There is no love like our God!

Praise Sentences (1 Samuel 2)

Rejoice in the Lord!
Find strength in God's promised love and hope!
Rejoice in the Lord!
Rejoice in the Lord!

NOVEMBER 22, 2009

Christ the King/Reign of Christ Sunday
B. J. Beu

COLOR
White

SCRIPTURE READINGS
2 Samuel 23:1-7; Psalm 132:1-12; Revelation 1:4b-8; John 18:33-37

THEME IDEAS
Kingship, both human and divine, focuses today's readings. Though a flawed vessel, King David was everything a human king ought to be. Second Samuel relates the last words of David, an oracle proclaiming the commitment of his house and lineage to God's everlasting covenant. David trusted the Lord. In Psalm 132, David forswears sleep until a resting place is found for the ark of the covenant. Yet, even David's piety, and God's promise of an everlasting covenant, cannot keep David's line from falling into sin. Divine kingship alone is sufficient to remain faithful. The readings from Revelation 1 and John 18 herald this kingship. Ultimately, all human kings fail us. Christ alone is our rightful King and Sovereign.

INVITATION AND GATHERING

Call to Worship (2 Samuel 23, John 18)

Christ came to be our King.
We have come to be Christ's people.
The King of kings calls us to follow him.
We have come to be Christ's people.
Christ came to be our King.
We have come to be Christ's people.

Opening Prayer (2 Samuel 23, Revelation 1)

Mighty Sovereign,
    we approach your throne
        to behold your glory.
Open our eyes,
    that we might witness your Son
        coming with the clouds
        to rule with justice
          and righteousness.
Open our hearts,
    that we may rejoice
        in your covenant,
        like the sun rising
          on a cloudless morning. Amen.

PROCLAMATION AND RESPONSE

Prayer of Confession (John 18, Revelation 1)

Almighty God,
    we are intoxicated by power—
        the power to dominate,
        the power to control,
        the power to punish,
        the power to reward,
        the power to have our own way.
We live in a powerful country
    with powerful leaders
        and a powerful military.

Forgive us when we lose sight
  of what true power is all about.
Forgive us when we forget
  that Jesus is our true and only King.
Help us refasten our gaze on Christ's kingdom,
  that we might work
  to bring this kingdom here on earth.
In the name of the Alpha and Omega,
  the first and the last, we pray. Amen.

Words of Assurance (Psalm 132)

The Lord made a covenant with King David,
  promising faithfulness to his descendants.
In Christ, we have a new covenant,
  assuring us forgiveness of sins
    and fullness of grace.
In Christ, our true king,
  our lives are made whole.

Response to the Word (2 Samuel 23)

The spirit of the Lord speaks to us,
  teaching us lessons that endure.
The Light of light shines on us,
  illuminating the minds of the wise.
The spirit of the Lord speaks to us,
  leading us into life.
This is the word of God for the people of God.
  Thanks be to God!

Call to Prayer (Revelation 1)

The Alpha and Omega, the first and last, the one who was
and is and is to come, is the Lord God Almighty. Let us
lift up our prayers to the one who offers us every blessing.

THANKSGIVING AND COMMUNION

Invitation to the Offering (2 Samuel 23)

Rock of Israel,
  you bless us with the light of morning,

the sun dawning on a new day;
you grace us with dew on the grass,
    the glistening promise of new possibilities.
Open our eyes to your splendor,
    and open our hearts to our call
        to give of ourselves
            each and every day.

SENDING FORTH

Benediction (2 Samuel 23, Psalm 132, Revelation 1)

The mighty one of Jacob sends us forth.
We go with God's blessing.
The rock of Israel sends us forth.
We go with God's blessing.
The Alpha and Omega sends us forth.
We go with God's blessing.

CONTEMPORARY OPTIONS

Contemporary Gathering Words

Our leaders always fail us.
Follow Christ, our Lord, our King.
Our leaders always let us down.
Follow Christ, our Lord, our King.
Our leaders always lose their way.
Follow Christ, our Lord, our King.

Praise Sentences (John 18)

Our king has come.
Worship Christ the king.
Our king has come.
Worship Christ the king.
Our king has come.

NOVEMBER 26, 2009

Thanksgiving Day
Mary J. Scifres

COLOR
Red or White

SCRIPTURE READINGS
Joel 2:21-27; Psalm 126; 1 Timothy 2:1-7; Matthew 6:25-33

THEME IDEAS
Rejoice and give thanks! This is a day to remember the gifts and blessings that God showers in our lives. This is a season to trust in God's providential care and to rest assured that we are held in Christ's gentle arms of love. In those arms, we have everything we need. In a world that instills fear and worry that nothing we have will ever be enough, we discover in Christ's care that we have everything we need, and indeed it is enough.

INVITATION AND GATHERING

Call to Worship (Joel 2, Psalm 126)
Be glad and rejoice!
    We rejoice in God's gifts!
Sing praises of joy!
    Our mouths are filled with laughter.
With gratitude, we come.
    God has done great things for us.

Shout with laughter, in sunshine and rain.
Praise God for our lives, for harvest and food.

Opening Prayer (Joel 2, Matthew 6)
O Giver of life,
  we thank you for the many ways
    you care for us,
    blessing us with abundance.
For sunshine and showers,
  we give you thanks.
For food and drink,
  we give you praise.
For clothing and shelter,
  we bestow our gratitude.
As we gather to give you thanks this day,
  gather our worries and our burdens.
Shelter us from fear and despair.
Help us rest in your arms,
  assured that your loving care is enough.
It is enough.
It is enough. Amen.

PROCLAMATION AND RESPONSE

Prayer of Confession (Psalm 126, Matthew 6)
God of abundant love,
  fill us with your joy
    even when we remember times
      of sin and sorrow.
Sprinkle the tears that we have sown
  with your mercy and hope,
    that we may reap a harvest of joy.
Forgive our fears and our worries.
Instill trust within us,
  that we may truly rest in your arms
    and have faith in your gracious care.
Forgive us when we are seduced
  by the accumulation of things

for which we have no need.
Comfort us when we worry over things
    for which we have no control.
Forgive us when we dream of wealth and prestige
    and forget that the necessities of life are enough.
Turn our dreams to you, O Lord.
Remind us of the abundance you offer
    as we proclaim today and forever:
        "God has done great things for us.
        Our tears are turned into joy!"

Words of Assurance (Psalm 126, Matthew 6)

Indeed, God has done great things for us.
Through Christ, God's love and grace
    are restored in our lives
        and we are made whole yet again.

Passing the Peace of Christ (1 Timothy 2, Matthew 6)

Share with one another signs of peace and love. Show
Christ to one another, that we may be reminded of the
peace that passes all understanding.

Response to the Word

This is a day to remember the gifts and blessings that God
showers in our lives. This is a season to trust in God's
providential care and to rest assured that we are held in
Christ's gentle arms of love. In those arms, we have everything we need. In a world that instills fear and worry that
nothing we have will ever be enough, we discover in
Christ's care that we have everything we need, and indeed it is enough. Rejoice and give thanks!

THANKSGIVING AND COMMUNION

Invitation to the Offering (Joel 2, Thanksgiving)

Be glad and rejoice! Summer has brought green forests
and sunny days. Fall now brings abundant fields and
changing leaves. As the rain falls upon us, may we remember that the seasons, the fertile earth, and the blessings

they yield are gifts from God. Be glad and rejoice, as we now return God's gifts to Christ and Christ's church.

Call to Prayer (1 Timothy 2)

I urge you, sisters and brothers, to bring your supplications, prayers, intercessions, and thanksgiving to God.

Prayer of Thanksgiving (Joel 2, 1 Timothy 2, Matthew 6, Thanksgiving)

Giver of life,
    we thank you for the gifts of sunshine and rain,
    the gifts of summer and fall.
For the coming winter and the change of seasons,
    we give you thanks.
For the blessings of our lives
    and the opportunities to experience joy,
    we give you praise.
Even as we thank you and return gifts to you,
    we remember that many are in need
    of your love and care.
Help us worry more for others
    than we do for ourselves.
Be with those who struggle for daily needs.
Empower those who live in fear and violence.
Encourage those who suffer in sorrow and despair.
Guide our leaders and our nation
    as we strive to welcome your presence on this earth
    and to create the world that you proclaim
    in your Son, Jesus Christ.
Restore our fortunes, O Lord—
    not the fortunes of money and power,
    but the fortunes of love and mercy,
    the gifts of grace and peace.
Strengthen us as we strive
    for your kingdom and your righteousness
    in our lives.
In Christ's name, we pray. Amen.

SENDING FORTH

Benediction (Psalm 126, Matthew 6)
Go forth with shouts of joy!
Proclaim the greatness of God!
Be glad and rejoice in Christ's care.
Trust that God goes with us!

CONTEMPORARY OPTIONS

Contemporary Gathering Words (Psalm 126, Matthew 6, Advent)
When God restored the fortunes of Zion,
the Israelites wandered home as if in a dream.
When Christ's birth was announced to Mary and Joseph,
they wandered to Bethlehem as if in a dream.
When Jesus proclaimed God's care
for even the birds and flowers of the earth,
we wander in fields of wonder.
Wander amongst God's marvelous creation!
Wonder at the amazing things God has done!
Do not worry about your life, today or tomorrow.
Trust instead that Christ will walk with us,
whatever life brings.
Trust that God values us even more greatly
than birds and flowers,
no matter how beautiful they may be.
Know that God treasures us completely,
and gives us all that we will ever need.

Praise Sentences (Joel 2)
Be glad! Rejoice in God!
We are glad to rejoice in God!
God has done great things for us!
We are glad to rejoice in God!

NOVEMBER 29, 2009

First Sunday of Advent

B. J. Beu

COLOR
Purple

SCRIPTURE READINGS
Jeremiah 33:14-16; Psalm 25:1-10; 1 Thessalonians 3:9-13;
Luke 21:25-36

THEME IDEAS
The promised one of God is coming. Jeremiah foretold of
a "righteous Branch" that would spring up for David.
Luke speaks of Jesus as the Son of Man who is coming in
clouds of glory. Whatever title we use, God's promised
one will execute justice and bring salvation to God's people. Be alert, therefore, for redemption draws near.

INVITATION AND GATHERING

Call to Worship (Jeremiah 33, Psalm 25)
The days are surely coming, says the Lord,
when I will cause a righteous Branch to spring forth
and bring my promised salvation to Israel.
   The Lord is our righteousness.
The days are surely coming, says our God,
when justice and mercy will be executed
throughout the land.

The Lord is our righteousness.
The days are surely coming, says the Lord,
when my promised one will teach transgressors my ways,
and heal the world with love and mercy.
The Lord is our righteousness.

Opening Prayer (Psalm 25, Luke 21)

Righteous one,
   to you alone
      we lift our souls;
   in you alone
      we place our trust;
   for you alone
      we wait all day long.
For you are the God
   of our salvation,
   abounding in mercy
      and steadfast love.
Help us remain alert and watchful
   for the coming of your promised one—
      the one who comes with power and glory,
      the one drawing near
to bring our salvation. Amen.

PROCLAMATION AND RESPONSE

Prayer of Confession (Luke 21)

Almighty God,
   you warn us to read the signs
      for the coming of your glory—
         in the sun, the moon, the stars,
         the roaring of the seas and the waves,
         the distress among the nations.
We have seen it all before.
Nothing seems to change.
Help us live with courage
   in this age of ambiguity
      where wars are fought for peace

and freedoms are stripped
in the name of liberty.
Forgive our lapse of focus,
our sense that nothing ever really changes.
Teach us to wait with patience,
that we may be ready
as our redeemer draws near. Amen.

Words of Assurance (Jeremiah 33, Psalm 25, Luke 21)
From of old, our God is a God of mercy,
abounding in steadfast love.
When we return to the Lord with our whole heart,
God will remember our sins no more.
In the name of God's righteous branch,
the Son of Man, the one who draws near,
we are forgiven.

Invitation to the Word (Psalm 25)
Make your ways known, O Lord;
teach us your paths.
Lead us into your truth and instruct our hearts—
for you are the God of our salvation;
for you we wait all day long.

Call to Prayer (1 Thessalonians 3, Luke 21)
Just as Paul prayed night and day to meet face to face with
the Thessalonians, that he might restore whatever was
lacking in their faith, so Christ invites us to be alert at all
times, praying that we may have the strength to stand true
before the Son of Man. Let us offer our prayers to the one
who promises us eternal life.

THANKSGIVING AND COMMUNION

Invitation to the Offering (Psalm 25)
The paths of the Lord are steadfast love and faithfulness
for those who keep God's covenant and decrees. God
leads the humble in what is right. It is right to share our
blessing in a world where justice for many is still but a

dream, and mercy is but a hope seen from afar. With
thankful hearts, let us share our gifts out of gratitude for
the joy of God's kingdom in our lives.

SENDING FORTH

Benediction (1 Thessalonians 3:12-13)
May the Lord make you increase and abound
in love for one another and for all,
just as Christ abounds in love for you.
And may the Lord strengthen your hearts in holiness,
that you may be blameless before God
at the coming of our Lord Jesus.

CONTEMPORARY OPTIONS

Contemporary Gathering Words (Luke 21)
Christ draws near.
A new day is dawning.
God's kingdom is here.
A new day is dawning.
It's time to wake up.
A new day is dawning.
Christ draws near.
A new day is dawning.

Praise Sentences (Jeremiah 33)
The Lord is our righteousness.
Redemption draws near.
The Lord is our righteousness.
The kingdom of God is near.
The Lord is our righteousness.
Christ's salvation is at hand.

DECEMBER 6, 2009

Second Sunday of Advent
Bill Hoppe

COLOR
Purple

SCRIPTURE READINGS
Malachi 3:1-4; Luke 1:68-79; Philippians 1:3-11; Luke 3:1-6

THEME IDEAS
The exhortation to "prepare the way of the Lord" echoed in the ears of God's people through the centuries and stands center stage in today's readings from Malachi and Luke. Despite these urgings and warnings, the world was taken by surprise on the day that Christ appeared. John the Baptist was sent as a herald and a messenger to prepare for the Lord's coming, and the Holy Spirit prepares a place in our hearts for the appearance of God's love and presence in our lives. The passage from Philippians assures us that whether we're ready or not, the one who started this amazing work will surely bring it to completion in each of us "for the glory and praise of God."

INVITATION AND GATHERING

Call to Worship (Luke 1, 3)
A voice cries out in the wilderness:
"Prepare the way of the Lord!"

Make God's paths straight.
Every valley will be filled,
and every mountain will be leveled.
The crooked will be made straight.
The rough and rocky ways will be smoothed.
All will see the salvation of God.
See the light from on high.
The dawn is breaking.
The Lord is coming! The Lord is coming!

Opening Prayer (Malachi 3)

Blessed is the Lord,
 and blessed are God's people
  to whom God sends a savior, the messiah,
   who is Christ the Lord.
Blessed is our God,
 and blessed are God's gifts,
  that grace us with forgiveness
  and every good gift.
Lord, you have come to dwell within us.
Build your temple within our hearts. Amen.

PROCLAMATION AND RESPONSE

Prayer of Confession (Malachi 3; Luke 1, 3)

O Lord,
 darkness surrounds us
  like a cold stone tomb,
  until your light bursts into our lives
   like a clear, bright dawn.
We cover our eyes,
 we're so unprepared for your coming.
Your light blazes forth like a white-hot fire,
 consuming all that it touches.
How can we stand before you, Lord?
The road that we thought was straight and wide
 is now exposed as a twisted, crooked path,
  blocked by a mountain of sin.

Where can we turn?
Who will guide us back to the way of peace—
    the way that leads to you?

Words of Assurance (Luke 1, Malachi 3, Philippians 1)

The Lord is merciful and forgiving,
    a great and compassionate savior.
God rescues us from darkness
    and frees us from fear.
Like a refiner's fire, the Lord makes us shine
    with the brilliance of the purest gold and silver.
The one who began this work in us
    seeks to bring it to completion.
May the day of Christ find us flawless
    and without blame.

Passing the Peace of Christ (Philippians 1)

Look around. This place is filled with those who thank
God every time they think of you. By the Lord's grace and
compassion, this place is filled with those who hold you
in their hearts, those whose prayers for you are filled with
joy. Share the peace of Christ Jesus with one another.

Response to the Word (Philippians 1)

Living Word of God,
    live within us,
    live within our hearts.
Let your light and love
    overflow more and more each day
        as we await your coming. Amen.

THANKSGIVING AND COMMUNION

Invitation to the Offering (Malachi 3, Luke 1)

The Lord is coming. Prepare the way! Prepare to welcome
the messiah! Welcome the redeemer with your very lives.
Know the Lord's tender mercy. Let all that you are become
an offering pleasing to God.

Offering Prayer (Luke 1)

We delight in your love and salvation, Lord,
  there can be no greater gifts than these.
We will gladly serve you
  in holiness and righteousness.
We offer ourselves.
We offer all that you have provided us.
May it be used to bring your light
  to those who dwell in darkness.
Prepare us and complete us, Lord. Amen.

SENDING FORTH

Benediction (Philippians 1)

May your love overflow,
  rich and wholesome in the world.
May you be found pure and blameless,
  having prepared a way and a place
    for the Lord in your hearts.
May you reap the bountiful harvest of righteousness
  that comes through Jesus Christ,
  to the glory and praise of God. Amen.

CONTEMPORARY OPTIONS

Contemporary Gathering Words (Malachi 3, Luke 1)

The messenger of God's holy covenant is coming!
  Prepare the way of the Lord!
The messenger comes to prepare the way before us!
  Prepare the way of the Lord!
Who can endure, who can stand when the Lord appears?
  Prepare the way of the Lord!

Praise Sentences (Luke 1)

The Lord has redeemed all people.
Blessed be the Lord God!
  The Lord has redeemed all people.
  Blessed be the Lord God!

DECEMBER 13, 2009

Third Sunday of Advent

Mary J. Scifres

COLOR
Purple

SCRIPTURE READINGS
Zephaniah 3:14-20; Isaiah 12:2-6; Philippians 4:4-7; Luke 3:7-18

THEME IDEAS
Rejoice! God is with us! These themes shout from today's Hebrew scripture lections and from Philippians 4. The gospel reading, however, differs markedly. John the Baptist has a more dour view on proclaiming the good news. This contrast reminds us that rejoicing in God's presence is truly joy only when we live as God's presence in the world. When we are a light to the nations, as God's people have always been called to be, we not only sing God's praises loudly and clearly for all to hear, we live God's promises righteously and lovingly for all to see and know.

INVITATION AND GATHERING

Call to Worship (Zephaniah 3, Isaiah 12)
Sing loudly with praise for God.
God is with us here!

Rejoice in the God of our salvation.
God is in our midst!

—Or—

Call to Worship

Sing aloud, sons and daughters!
Shout with joyful praise!
Rejoice in the Lord always.
Again we will say, "Rejoice!"
The God of our salvation is near at hand.
Our redeemer is in our midst.
With shouts of hope, we sing to God.
Again we sing, "Rejoice!"
Make known God's deeds.
Proclaim Christ's love for all to hear.
With hearts of laughter, we love.
Again we say, "Rejoice!"

Opening Prayer (Zephaniah 3, Isaiah 12)

With laughing hearts and joyous hope,
  we come to you, O God.
With tired souls and withered dreams,
  we come to you, O God.
In our joy and in our sorrow,
  we turn to you, O God.
Renew us with your love.
Gather us into your strong embrace,
  that we may know your presence
  and rejoice in your promised coming.
With hopeful expectation, we pray. Amen.

PROCLAMATION AND RESPONSE

Prayer of Confession (Zephaniah 3, Luke 3, Advent)

Come, Lord Jesus.
Come quickly into our lives
  and into our hearts.
Renew us with your love.

Help us bear fruit
worthy of repentance.
Where there is hatred,
heal us with your love.
Where there is discord,
calm us with your peace.
Where there is sin,
cover us with your grace.
Where there is despair,
strengthen us with your hope.
Baptize us with the fire of your Holy Spirit,
that we may be refined
and cleansed of our sins.
Gather us into your midst,
that we may be your people.
Amen and amen.

Words of Assurance (Zephaniah 3, Philippians 4)
Do not fear, dear children of God,
for God is in our midst.
Christ has taken away all judgments against us,
and we are forgiven and reconciled to God.
Rejoice! Again, I say, rejoice!

Passing the Peace of Christ
Let us share together signs of the peace of God—the peace
that passes all understanding, the peace that overcomes
all divisions. The peace of Christ be with you.
And also with you.

Response to the Word or Invitation to the Offering
We have heard the word preached and proclaimed.
What then shall we do?
Be satisfied with what you have been given.
Whoever has two coats shall share with anyone
who has none.
What more must we do?
Must we sell all that we have
and give it to the poor?

Trust your heart to know what is right.
Abundant God,
in this time of buying and selling,
accumulating and overindulgence,
draw us closer to you.
Help us share out of our abundance.
Help us proclaim your good news
in our words and in our actions.
Baptize us with your love,
that we may be your loving presence
in the world. Amen.

THANKSGIVING AND COMMUNION

Invitation to Communion (Zephaniah 3, Luke 3)
Come to the table of grace. Partake in the bread of life. All are welcome here—for Christ gathers us in, transforming chaff into wheat, forgiving sins with great mercy, and overcoming death with new life. Come! Be satisfied with the gracious gifts of God.

Prayer of Thanksgiving (Zephaniah 3, Isaiah 12)
With joyous gladness,
we thank you for these gifts of grace.
For gathering us in when we were outcast,
we give you thanks and praise.
For saving us when we were lost and lame,
we are ever grateful.
For loving us and being present with us,
we thank you.
May the nourishment we have found at your table
strengthen us to proclaim your name
and make known your deeds
to all people in all times and places. Amen.

SENDING FORTH

Benediction (Philippians 4)
And now, may the peace of God
that passes all understanding

be with you now and forevermore.
Rejoice in God always!
Again, I say, rejoice!

CONTEMPORARY OPTIONS

Contemporary Gathering Words (Zephaniah 3, Isaiah 12)
Shout to the Lord! Sing aloud to God!
God is with us now.
Sing of God's deeds. Speak of Christ's grace.
God is with us here.
Live as God's people. Walk in God's ways.
God is with us on the way.

Praise Sentences (Zephaniah 3, Philippians 4, Advent)
Christ is near.
Rejoice and sing!
Sing aloud to God!
Christ is near.
Rejoice and sing!
Sing aloud to God!

DECEMBER 20, 2009

Fourth Sunday of Advent
Laura Jaquith Bartlett

COLOR
Purple

SCRIPTURE READINGS
Micah 5:2-5a; Luke 1:46b-55; Hebrews 10:5-10; Luke 1:39-45

THEME IDEAS
When we join with Mary in singing the Magnificat, we're not just singing another carol to pass the time till Christmas arrives—we're celebrating the impending arrival of the one who turns the world upside down! From the tiny hamlet of Bethlehem comes the greatest gift ever. From the barren womb of Elizabeth comes the radical prophet and baptizer. From the mouth of a young, unmarried girl comes words of unswerving commitment, and a song of praise for the fulfillment of God's promises. For a church that has been lulled into complacency by too many warm, familiar Christmas rituals, these Advent readings offer shocking witness that the kingdom of God is indeed at hand.

INVITATION AND GATHERING

Call to Worship (Micah 5, Luke 1)
God has done great things for us!
God's love is heralded in the promise of Christ.

Holy is God's name!
God's promises are fulfilled in the coming of Christ.
God's mercy extends from generation to generation.
God's salvation is offered in the gift of Christ.

Opening Prayer (Micah 5, Luke 1)

Holy God,
    your prophet Micah foretold with faith
        that a new ruler would come forth from Bethlehem—
            today we celebrate the fulfillment of your promise;
    your daughter Elizabeth proclaimed with faith
        that her cousin was to be the mother of her Lord—
            today we celebrate the fulfillment of your promise;
    your servant Mary proclaimed with faith
        that she would be called blessed by all generations—
            today we celebrate the fulfillment of your promise.
Make us bold enough to proclaim with faith—
    the coming of your kingdom,
    the coming of your justice,
    the coming of your peace.
May we sing out the good news of your salvation,
    trusting in fulfillment of your promises.
All this we pray in the name of the one who comes.
Amen.

PROCLAMATION AND RESPONSE

Prayer of Confession (Micah 5, Luke 1)

Loving God,
    even in the midst of this season of goodwill,
        there is much to confess.
In spite of holiday cheer,
    stress and anxiety rule our lives.
We miss the reason for the season,
    focusing instead on Christmas parties, long to-do lists,
        and trying to get the shopping done.
We fail to think about your reordered world—
    a world where the lowly are lifted up

and the hungry are filled with good things.
Help us adjust our Christmas priorities,
   that we might join with you, O God,
     in preparing a world that welcomes
      the one who brings us peace.
(Prayer continues in silence.)

Words of Assurance

The ancient promises of God are fulfilled.
God does not forget us.
God's mercy extends from generation to generation.
Let our souls rejoice in God!

Invitation to the Word

*(This short dialogue for two women is followed by a congrega-
tional response. The response could be repeated at the conclusion of the sermon. The dialogue may be presented either before
or after the gospel reading.)*
(Mary knocks.)

Elizabeth: Mary!

Mary: Hello, Elizabeth. I greet you in the name of God.

Elizabeth: Mary, I greet you in the name of the One who is my Lord, the One you carry in your womb.

Mary: How could you know this?

Elizabeth: The Holy Spirit has shown me that God's promises have been fulfilled through you. Your faith has enabled God to work through you to bring about the peace we have longed for.

Mary: The Spirit has shown you the truth. I have been blessed beyond my wildest dreams, for God has chosen me to help birth those dreams we all have for justice and peace.

People: Holy Spirit, come and fill us with faith so that we, too, might work with God to bring about the coming of the One who brings us peace.

THANKSGIVING AND COMMUNION

Invitation to the Offering

In response to the news that she would bear God's Son, Mary offered herself as God's servant, and then sang a song celebrating her selection to help bring God's realm on earth. We have been chosen to continue to build up the kingdom of God, so we, too, have reason to celebrate. Having praised God through song and scripture, let us now offer our tangible signs of gratitude, confident that God's promises will be fulfilled through the ministries supported by our gifts.

Offering Prayer

Dear God,
> you blessed Mary
>> by making her the mother of your only Son,
>>> Jesus Christ.

You have blessed us, as well,
> with the gift of your Son,
> and indeed, with the gift of life itself.

Out of all these blessings,
> we give you back these offerings this day.

Knowing that your promises will be fulfilled,
> we pledge our lives to you
>> in anticipation of the coming of the one
>>> who brings us peace. Amen.

SENDING FORTH

Benediction

As we head into the final days before Christmas,
> may we leave this place secure in the knowledge
>> that God's promises will be fulfilled.

December 25 is just five days away,
> but the gift that God gives us
>> will not wear out or fade away.

—Or—

Go with the love of God,
   who extends mercy from generation to generation.
Go with the illumination of the Holy Spirit,
   who prepares us for the coming of our Lord.
Go with the peace of the Christ child,
   who comes to partner with us
      to bring the kingdom that will never end. Amen.

CONTEMPORARY OPTIONS

Contemporary Gathering Words

Blessed is tiny Bethlehem, from which shall come
the ruler of Israel.
**Blessed is Mary, who believed in the fulfillment
of God's word.**
Blessed is the One who comes in the name of the Lord.
Blessed is God, who gives us the gift of peace.

Praise Sentences (Luke 1:46b-55 Message)

Mary said, "I'm bursting with God-news;
I'm dancing the song of my Savior God....
What God has done for me will never be forgotten,
The God whose very name is holy,
   set apart from all others.
His mercy flows in wave after wave."
Let us all join with Mary,
   in dancing the song of our Savior God!

DECEMBER 24, 2009

Christmas Eve
Joanne Carlson Brown

COLOR
White

SCRIPTURE READINGS
Isaiah 9:2-7; Psalm 96; Titus 2:11-14; Luke 2:1-20

THEME IDEAS
The magic of this night is the magic of promises fulfilled: the magic of light bursting on darkness, the magic of a baby's cry and a mother's tender love, the magic of angels singing glorias to shepherds, the magic of God coming to earth to dwell among us. It is important to keep hold of this sense of magic as we tell the old familiar story from passages people know by heart. Something special, something incredible happens tonight. Rejoice, for our salvation has come!

INVITATION AND GATHERING

Call to Worship
A light shining in the darkness ...
> **What could it be?**

The sound of angels' wings ...
> **What could it mean?**

A baby born in a stable ...

Who could it be?
Come to Bethlehem and see.

Opening Prayer
O wondrous God of the stars,
    we come tonight with breathless wonder
        to see the babe who will change our lives.
We hear the names "Wonderful Counselor,"
    "Mighty God," "Prince of Peace,"
        and we are in awe.
You have touched the earth this night
    with your unconditional love.
Touch us—
    touch our hearts and minds and souls.
May we never tire of this story.
May we never take it for granted.
Make this night magical again. Amen.

PROCLAMATION AND RESPONSE

Prayer of Confession
It's Christmas Eve again, God.
We're barely ready for it.
So much to do to get ready—
    gifts to buy and wrap, parties to attend,
    trees to trim, houses to decorate.
We're in a whirlwind of activity.
In the midst of the busyness
    we sometimes miss what it is all about—
        you coming to earth—Emmanuel—God-with-us.
Help us hear anew
    your promises of hope and salvation and love
        as we sing our familiar carols.
Forgive us for forgetting the magic of this night,
    for focusing on ourselves and what we need to do
        instead of on the miracle of Jesus' birth.
Rock us out of our complacency.
Let us hear angel voices,

see shepherds hurrying to a stable,
feel the baby's soft breath on our cheeks,
and ponder in our hearts what all this means
for the world, for us.

Words of Assurance

God's love knows no bounds.
Love comes down at Christmas—
a love so deep and so profound
that nothing will ever be the same again.
Know that this love is come for you—
to touch you, to heal you, to forgive you,
to make you whole.

Passing the Peace of Christ

This night no one is a stranger. All are joined together as one family through the miracle of the birth of one small baby. Let us share our joy and excitement at being present when God reaches down to touch the earth. Let us reach out and touch each other in love incarnate.

Response to the Word

God, we see your light shining in the darkness.
We hear the Christmas Angels.
We behold your promises fulfilled
in the birth of this wondrous child.
May this magical story become real in our lives.

THANKSGIVING AND COMMUNION

Invitation to the Offering

Come now and kneel before the Christ child. Bring all that you are and all that you have. Offer your gifts in wonder and surprise and awe. Offer your gifts in joy and delight.

Invitation to Communion

This is a magical night. God-with-us has come to touch our world, our lives. God-with-us has come to bring us out of darkness into a glorious light. God-with-us invites us now to come to the table, believing in the promises of

God fulfilled tonight. Here we hear angels, and see shepherds, and are transformed by a baby. Here love is offered, and love is found, in the sharing of bread and cup. Here we find our journey's end and its beginning.

Offering Prayer
There are so many things
    to be thankful for tonight, God.
Receive these tokens of our gratitude
    for your love incarnate
        in the babe of Bethlehem.
May they become God-with-us for all the world.
May they breathe magic back into a world
    that needs a sense of wonder and joy.

SENDING FORTH

Benediction
Go now in wonder.
Go to bring light to those in darkness,
    joy to those who can find no joy,
    magic to a world steeped in realism.
Go with the songs of angels in your ears,
    and the love of God in your hearts.
Go and spread the word—
    the babe of Bethlehem is born for all.

CONTEMPORARY OPTIONS

Contemporary Gathering Words
Welcome to this most magical night
when angels and shepherds mingle
and the birth of a baby changes the world.
    We come to celebrate with joy and wonder.
Celebrate the light that shines all around us.
    We will sing and praise our most wondrous God.
Let us kneel before the Christ child,
who makes God's promises come true.

Praise Sentences
Unto us a child is born.
Unto us a child is given.
Wonderful Counselor, Mighty God, Prince of Peace.
Glory to God in the Highest!

DECEMBER 27, 2009

First Sunday after Christmas
Mary J. Scifres

COLOR
White

SCRIPTURE READINGS
1 Samuel 2:18-20, 26; Psalm 148; Colossians 3:12-17; Luke 2:41-52

THEME IDEAS
In Colossians 3, we see what it truly means to grow in wisdom and favor with God. To be mature in Christ is to be clothed in compassion, to be filled with love and kindness, and to be ready with forgiveness and patience. As the busy month of December comes to a close, and as we face hopes and fears for the new year, these scriptures remind us of the true gift of Christmas: the birth of love in our lives. To grow in compassion and kindness is to grow in the wisdom of God.

INVITATION AND GATHERING

Call to Worship (Psalm 148)
Praise God in the highest heavens!
  Praise God in the deepest seas!
All creation proclaims God's glory—
  sun and moon, snow and frost.

With birds and beasts, we sing God's praises.
With mountains and hills, we display God's glory.
Glory to God in the highest!
And peace to all on God's earth.

Opening Prayer (Colossians 3)
Ever-present God,
clothe us with your compassion.
Instill in us
your kindness and mercy.
Bind us together
in humble patience
and gentle love.
Rule in our hearts,
that we may be Christlike,
displaying your glory
in every word,
in every deed.
In the name of Christ Jesus,
we pray. Amen.

PROCLAMATION AND RESPONSE

Prayer of Confession (Colossians 3)
God of wisdom and grace,
guide us to be a people
of compassion and kindness.
When we clothe ourselves in sin,
forgive us.
When we separate ourselves
from you and your people,
bind us together as one.
When we withhold forgiveness or harbor hatred,
cover us with your mercy,
that we may be bound together in love
and be guided into your perfect harmony.
May your peace rule in our hearts,
and your forgiveness flow through our lives.

Clothe us in the mercy and patience
  we so desperately seek,
    in the name of Jesus Christ. Amen.

Words of Assurance (Colossians 3)
If anyone has a complaint against another,
  let forgiveness be our way.
For just as the Lord has forgiven us,
  so must we also forgive.
Receive the forgiveness Christ offers.
We are forgiven and reconciled to God.

Passing the Peace of Christ (Colossians 3)
Let us share God's forgiveness and reconciliation
  with one another.
Share now signs of peace and harmony,
  that we may be bound together in love.

Invitation to the Word (Colossians 3)
As God's chosen ones, holy and beloved, let us hear the words of scripture this day. May these words become meaningful in our lives, so that the very presence of Christ will dwell in us richly. May these words become ones we share together, teaching and admonishing us in God's wisdom. And may these words guide us to be both hearers and doers of the word, doing everything in the name of Jesus Christ.

THANKSGIVING AND COMMUNION

Invitation to the Offering (1 Samuel 2, Luke 2)
Hannah prayed for the blessing of a child, and Samuel was given to her. She returned the gift to God, dedicating Samuel to service in the temple, visiting him only once a year, bringing him a new robe to fit his quickly-growing body. Mary was blessed with the baby Jesus, a miraculous gift from God. And yet, this gift was not only to her, but to all the world. May we recognize the many gifts in our lives, and return now the gifts that our world so desperately needs.

Offering Prayer (Christmas, Colossians 3)

Gracious God,
> we come with gratitude and wonder
>> for your marvelous gifts.

We thank you for the blessing
> of Christ's birth on this earth—
>> the blessing of Christ's presence in our lives,
>> the presence of Christ in this church family,
>> and the opportunity to be the presence of Christ
>>> in your world.

Receive the gifts we now bring
> to you and your church.

Clothe these gifts with your love,
> even as you clothe us with compassion,
> that our lives and these gifts
>> may be transformed into your presence
>>> in our world. Amen.

SENDING FORTH

Benediction (1 Samuel 2, Psalm 148, Luke 2)

Like Samuel and Jesus before us,
> may we continue to grow both in stature and wisdom.

Like Samuel and Jesus before us,
> may our light shine for all to see.

May we be stars of praise, displaying God's glory,
> as we reflect Christ's love.

CONTEMPORARY OPTIONS

Contemporary Gathering Words (Colossians 3)

With gratitude and joy, come sing to the Lord.
> **With songs of praise, we come.**

With thankfulness and cheer, lift hymns to God on high.
> **With songs of praise, we come.**

With hope and joyful hearts, sing to Christ our King.
> **With songs of praise, we come.**

Praise Sentences (Psalm 148)

Praise God from the heavens.
Praise God from the heights!
Praise now the Lord!
Praise God with the angels.
Praise God with the stars.
Praise now the Lord!
Praise God with the mountains.
Praise God with the snow.
Praise now the Lord!
Praise God, young and old.
Praise God, women and men.
Praise now the Lord!

CONTRIBUTORS

Erik J. Alsgaard, a United Methodist clergy member of the Detroit Annual Conference, serves as the Director of Communications for the Florida Annual Conference.

Laura Jaquith Bartlett is an ordained minister of music (United Methodist) in Oregon, where she and her husband and two daughters all enjoy Scandinavian folk dancing and eating gelato.

B. J. Beu is pastor of Fox Island United Church of Christ, near Gig Harbor, Washington. A graduate of Boston University and Pacific Lutheran University, B. J. has chaired the worship committee for the annual meeting of the Pacific Northwest Conference of the United Church of Christ.

Robert Blezard is pastor of Trinity Lutheran Church, Arendtsville, Pennsylvania, and a contributing editor of *The Lutheran,* the denominational magazine of the ELCA.

Mary Petrina Boyd is pastor of University Temple United Methodist Church in Seattle. She spends alternate summers working as an archaeologist in Jordan.

John A. Brewer serves as pastor of Faith United Methodist Church in Issaquah, Washington. Serving almost forty years in pastoral ministry, John is chair of the Conference Board of Discipleship.

Joanne Carlson Brown is a United Methodist minister serving United Church in University Place, Washington, a joint

UMC/UCC congregation. She delights in her congregation of loving and committed people and shares her life with her beloved fur person, the wee Westie, Thistle.

Linda K. Crowe is blessed to serve as pastor of Veradale United Church of Christ in Spokane Valley, Washington.

Shelley Cunningham serves as Pastor for Children, Youth, and Family Ministry at Christ the King Lutheran Church (ELCA) in New Brighton, Minnesota. She also writes for Luther Seminary's alumni magazine, *The Story,* and its on-line daily devotional, *God Pause.*

Rebecca J. Kruger Gaudino is a United Church of Christ minister in Portland, Oregon, where she teaches world religions and biblical studies, and writes for the Church.

Jamie D. Greening is the senior pastor of First Baptist Church, Port Orchard, Washington, where he makes his home with his wife and two daughters.

Hans Holznagel, a member of Archwood United Church of Christ in Cleveland, Ohio, has worked in news, public relations, mission education, and administration in the national ministries of the United Church of Christ for more than twenty years.

Bill Hoppe is the music coordinator and keyboardist for Bear Creek United Methodist Church in Woodinville, Washington, and is also a friend of Aslan. He thanks his family and friends for their continued love, support, and inspiration.

Sara Dunning Lambert is the worship coordinator at Bear Creek United Methodist Church, Woodinville, Washington.

Shari Jackson Monson enjoys serving on the worship team and senior leadership team at Chapel Hill Presbyterian Church (Gig Harbor, Washington) as Executive of Mission and Strategy.

Edward W. Paup serves as Resident Bishop for the Seattle Area of The United Methodist Church, which includes the Pacific Northwest and Alaska Missionary Conferences.

Ciona D. Rouse is a freelance writer in Nashville, Tennessee, and member of Belmont United Methodist Church.

Bryan Schneider-Thomas is pastor of Amble United Methodist Church near Howard City, Michigan, and also serves churches as a consultant in art and architecture.

Mary J. Scifres serves as a consultant in leadership, worship, and evangelism from her Gig Harbor home near Seattle, where she and her husband, B. J., reside with their son, Michael. Her books include *The United Methodist Music and Worship Planner,* its ecumenical counterpart, *Prepare!* and the worship evangelism book *Searching for Seekers.*

Jennifer Yocum is an ordained minister serving the United Church of Christ. Out of her experience that music draws the angels closer so they can join in the singing, she keeps a songwriter's ear to the language of worship.

SCRIPTURE INDEX / COMMUNION LITURGIES INDEX

Old Testament

Communion Liturgies

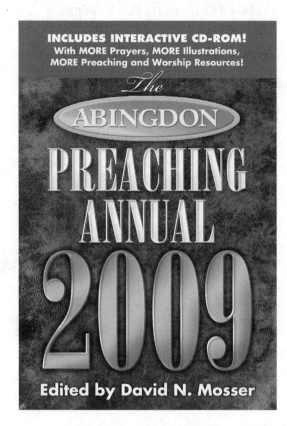

INCLUDES INTERACTIVE CD-ROM!
With MORE Prayers, MORE Illustrations,
MORE Preaching and Worship Resources!

The ABINGDON PREACHING ANNUAL 2009

Edited by David N. Mosser

Preachers have long turned to *The Abingdon Preaching Annual* for help with the central task of their ministry: sermon preparation. The 2009 edition of the *Annual* continues this fine tradition with lectionary-based and topical sermons for flexibility in choice, additional lectionary commentary, and worship aids for every sermon. The CD-ROM, included with every book, provides classical and contemporary affirmations and prayers, plus hyperlinked planning aids such as bibliographical references, and the full lectionary texts for each Sunday. *The Abingdon Preaching Annual* is now one of the most comprehensive and useful resources for sermon preparation that you will find on the market today.

"Commendations to Abingdon Press for offering two fresh ecumenical resources for pastors."

For *The Abingdon Preaching Annual*—"Anyone who dares proclaim a holy word week in and week out soon realizes that creative inspiration for toe-shaking sermons quickly wanes. Multitasking pastors who are wise seek out resources that multiply their own inductive initiatives."

For *The Abingdon Worship Annual*—"Not only the sermon but also the whole service dares to be toe-shaking . . . and the *Worship Annual* is a reservoir of resources in that direction."

—The Reverend Willard E. Roth, Academy of Parish Clergy President, *Sharing the Practice: The Journal of the Academy of Parish Clergy*

 Abingdon Press   w w w . c o k e s b u r y . c o m